ENGLISH RECUSANT LITERATURE
1558–1640

Selected and Edited by
D. M. ROGERS

Volume 213

PEDRO MOREION
A Briefe Relation of the
Persecution . . . in the Kingdome
of Japonia
1619

PEDRO MOREION
A Briefe Relation of the
Persecution . . . in the Kingdome
of Japonia
1619

The Scolar Press
1974

ISBN o 85967 197 6

Published and printed in Great Britain by
The Scolar Press Limited, 59-61 East Parade,
Ilkley, Yorkshire and
39 Great Russell Street,
London WC1

A BRIEFE
RELATION
OF THE PERSECVTION
LATELY MADE

Againſt the Catholike Chriſtians, in the
Kingdome of IAPONIA,

Deuided into two Bookes.

Taken out of the Annuall Letters of the Fathers of
the Society of IESVS, and other Authenticall
Informations. Written in Spaniſh, and printed firſt at *Mexico* in the Weſt Indies, the
yeare of Chriſt M. DC. XVI.

AND

Newly tranſlated into English by W. W. *Gent.*

THE FIRST PART.

Permiſſu Superiorum, M. DC. XIX.

The Contents.

IN this firſt Part is ſet downe what hap.
pened in *Iaponia*, before the baniſhment
thence of the Fathers of the Society of
IESVS, & other Religious Perſons, that
there preached the Chriſtian Fayth.

IN the ſecond, is declared what ſucceeded
after their departure.

TO ALL
THAT SVFFER
PERSECVTION
IN ENGLAND
FOR
CATHOLIKE RELIGION.

HIS enſuing Relation being ſent out of the *VVeſt Indies* where it was firſt printed to a friend of mine in *Spaine*, & from thence by him to me, after I had read & peruſed the ſame, it ſee-

med

medvnto me, &others alfo whofe iudgmentes I farre preferre before mine owne, to be worthy the publike view. Whereupon I refolued (though my neceffary occafions would fcarce affoard me leafure) to fteale fo much time from them as was neceffary for the tranflating it out of Spanish into our English tongue. More paynes and labour it coft me then at the firft I thought it would haue done: and I found therein that true by experience which I had often heard of others, to wit, that it is not fo eafy to tranflate out of one language into another, as is commonly imagined.

    Hauing at length finished the

the fame, I knew not to whome I
might better direct it, then to
You the poore afflicted Catholikes of this our Countrey, for
whofe comfort and encourage-
ment I did indeed principally
from the beginning intend it.
For although I do prefume it
wilbe gratefull to all Chriftians
of what nation or nature foeuer
they be, to vnderftand of the
propagation, increafe, and aug-
mentation of Chriftian Religion in thofe Countries where
before there was neuer any notice therof, and of the conftant
perfeuerance of thofe therein
that haue fo lately receiued and
imbraced it: yet am I certainly
perfwaded, that it wilbe to you
A 3   much

much more welcome, then to
any other;not only becaufe thefe
moft worthy Chriftiãs of *Iaponia*
wherof this relatiõ doth entreate
be of the fame Chriftian and
Catholike Fayth and Religon
that you be, and not of any o-
thér priuate or particular fect or
faction, of which God knoweth
there is to great a multitude in
the Chriftian world in thefe mi-
ferable dayes of ours: but alfo by
reafon of the great likeneffe and
fimilitude betwixt their cafe and
yours.

If it be an axiome in Philo-
fophy, that *Omne fimile gaudet fibi
fimili*, Euery thinge doth take
a particuler delight in fuch
thinges as be like vnto it felfe;
well

well may it be supposed that it
wilbe at least some kind of contentment vnto you (amongst so
many occasions of discomfort as
are dayly offered) to vnderstand
of the estate of those that in many thinges do more symbolize
with you, then any other persons
in the world . For (omitting
that they be Inhabitants of an
Iland as we be, and of the greatest Iland in those partes of the
world as we in these, of the like
Climate also that we be, all
thinges considered, they in a
manner Antipodes to vs, and
we to them) first of all they be
but lately conuerted to the
true faythof Christ from Infidelity , and so be most of you from

A 4   Schisme

Schifme or Herefy, which is a kind of infidelity : to them it is graūted according to the faying S. *Paul*, to fuffer for theyr faith; and fo it is to you : they be falfly flaundered and calumniated in many thinges by the Diuels minifters, and fo be you : they be perfecuted for theyr Religion, many of them to death & more to loffe of goods by the enemies of Chrift and his holy Church; and fo be you, very many amongft you hauing loft theyr liues, and more theyr goods & liuinges for no other caufe but only the conftant confeffion of the Catholike Religion. Finally they for theyr valour and conftancy in Gods caufe be famous

in

in all thofe partes of the world,
yea , and in Europe alfo ; and
you for yours be no leffe glóri-
ous, both in all Europe , and in
the reft of the Chriftian world :
fo that I may well fay both of
you and them , that which the
Apoftle fayd to the Romanes
(whofe religion both they and
you imbrace) *fides veſtra annun-*
tiatur in vniuerfo mundo , your conftancy in fayth is published and
famous throughout the whole
world .

    Thefe then be the reafons
for which I thought it moft
expedient to dedicate this short
Relation vnto You ; although
there wanteth not alfo another ,
which truly I muft needes con-
     A 5   feffe

felfe was of great force to moue
me thereunto : the which is that
I hoped thereby you would
both be more carefull to commend in your prayers to Almighty God the neceffities of
thofe poore afflicted Chriftians,
your Brethren, as alfo more
willing to imitate theyr admi-
rable examples of valour and
courage in the caufe of Chrift,
and of patience and conftancy in
enduring croffes and perfecutions, troubles and tribulations
for the fame. Many of you I
know haue oftentimes occafions
miniftred of fuffering wronges
and iniuries, loffes and difgraces
for the fame caufe, the fame
Fayth and Religion for which
they

they do endure all these cruell
persecutions . If then you do
imitate theyr patience, theyr
courage and constancy, theyr
ioyfulnes and alacrity therein,
you shall obteyne thereby the
like honour & renowne in earth
that they haue done, and afterwardes in their company euerlasting crownes of glory in heauen : for as the holy Apostle te-
stifyeth, *Si socij passionum estis, eritis
& consolationis* ; if you be partakers of theyr sufferinges, yee
shall also be companions of
theyr comfortes, ioyes, and consolations .

And because there be some
things in the discourse of this relation which proceding from an
extra-

extraordinary feruour, are rather
to be admired of all, then imita-
ted of any that is not after an
especiall manner moued by Almighty God, as we may prudēt-
ly iudge those persons were that
did them; I doubt not but that
you guided by discretion (reue-
rencing such like actions as is-
suing from the particuler mo-
tion and inspiration of the holy
Ghost) will apply your endeauours, only or principally, to
imitate those other thinges that
are more conformable to the
common course of vertuous and
pious persons ʿ assisted with the
grace of Christ; knowing that
thereby you shall both auoyd
the domage that is incident to
                            those

those that rashly thrust themselues into eminent dangers; &
also gaine withall no small merit
to you soules

It shall not be needfull for
me to aduertise you how this
persecution of the poore Christians of *Iapone* was partly, if not
principally, occasioned by persons of the same profession in
religion, as those be that persecute you:nor yet to note how like
the Diuell is vnto himselfe in all
places; causing the Gentiles
there to hate and exterminate
the pictures and images of our
Blessed Sauiour and his Saintes,
togeather with all other thinges
appertayning to the promotion
of Christian piety, as he hath
moued

moued your Perfecutors here
vtterly to abandon and abolish
them : It shall not I say be needfull for me, to signify thefe
thinges vnto you, for that I do
affure my felfe that your felues
in the reading thereof will eafily
obferue thefe and many other
thinges greatly worth the mar-
king; as the great feare and care
of the gentiles leaft any reliques
of the holy Martyrs should remaine to be reuerenced by the
deuouter fort of Chriftians :
theyr extraordinary diligence
to make thofe that were conftant
in theyr fayth, to diffemble at
leaft a little while in the exterior
profeffion thereof : they r falfe
and flaunderous calumniations
                              of

of the Catholike religion : theyr feares , suspitions, and iealosies of preists and religious persons concerning matters of State, all of them thinges common to them ,and to the Gentils of former times that persecuted Gods Church, as also to the Heritikes of all ages , and in especiall to these of ours .

That which I would wish you to reflect vpon , is only the bad successe euen in temporall affayres which in the end befell to such persons that for worldly respectes, eyther forsooke theyr religion, or without care of theyr conscience behaued themselues to the discredit therof: and how on the contrary those that were

constant

conſtant therein, and carefull to frame theyr liues according thereunto, beſides theyr hap-pines in heauen, & honour vpon earth, through the Paternall prouidence of Almighty God, were euer in the end after ſome ſuffering ſufficiently prouided for.

And now becauſe I do i-magin that many of you hither-to haue not had much notice of the Kingdome of *Iapone*, and leſſe of the affayres therof, it be-ing a country ſo farre diſtant & remote from ours, as perhaps few or none in the world more (at leaſt, as it is acceſſible) and by reaſon thereof you will not ſo eaſily vnderſtand ſome thinges that

that will occurre in the reading
of this relation : I haue therefore thought it not amisse
breifly by way of a Preface or In-
troduction to set downe some
few things concerning the same
that may help to giue you some
litle light therein . If therewith
or by the reading the relation it
selfe you shall receiue but so
much contentment as I tooke
paynes in the translating thereof, yea or but any confort or o-
ther good at all , I shall thinke
any labours very well bestowed,
desiring no other thinge in requitall thereof but only to be
remembred in your best deuoti-
ons, and made partaker of those
afflictions that it shall please

B   our

our Bleſſed Sauiour to giue
you grace to ſuffer for his ſake:
and ſo humbly beſeeching Almighty God to ſend you eyther
a ſpeedy end of them, or elſe
much patience to endure them
as long as it ſhall be his holy wil
and pleaſure to permit them,
with all dutifull reſpect I take
my leaue, euer remayning

> *Your ſeruant in Chriſt*
> *Ieſus*, W. W.

THE

THE
PREFACE TO
TH·E READER:

*A*MONGST *other coū-
tryes which were vn-
knowne to vs of* Europe
*vntill in this later age
they were difcouered by
the* Spaniardes *&* Por-
tugalls, *one is* Iaponẹ, *vnder which name
be contcyned diuers Ilandẹs lying in the eaſt
Ocean of the great Kingdome of* China,
a chiefe prouince of Aſia, *from whence the
neareſt of them is diſtant ſome nineſcore*
English *miles, and about foure hundred and
fifty from* Noua Eſpaña *a principall part
of the* Weſt Indies, *conquered and inhabited
by the* Spaniſh *Nation. Theſe Ilandes are*
B 2   *deuided*

deuided one from the other by litle crikes or
armes of the sea; and amongst them there
be three which do farre exceed the rest, vnto
the which the others are subiect, and in a
manner do adhere. The greatest of these
three, which is called Niphon, doth lye from
East to West, and is 700. miles in length and
180. in breadth, and it deuided into three &
fifty litle Kingdomes or Prouinces, and
therein is the noble Citty of Meaco the
chiefe and head of all Iapone. The second
called Ximo extendeth it selfe from North
to South, and hath in it nine Kingdomes.
The third Scicoco, is deiuded into foure
Prouinces, and lyeth Eastward from the second. All these Ilandes be for the most part
full of hilles and mountaines, much subiest
vnto could and raine, whereupon it proceedeth that for the most part they be nothing
fertile, rather subiect vnto barrennes. They
yeeld no wheate nor rye, nor any such like
graine, at least but very small: the chiefe
thinge they beare is rice, which they bring
forth in great aboundance: they haue the
same kind of birdes and beastes that we of
                                Europe,

Europe, both wild and tame, though the Inhabitantes seldome eate the flesh of any vnlesse at sometimes it be of Venison. Theyr common fare is hearbes, and fish, and ryce, of the which they also make a kind of wine, although theyr ordinary drinke be warme water into the which in feastes and banquets they put a certaine ponder much esteemed of them, the which is called Cha. Theyr buildings for the most part be of wood, partly because they haue but little store of stone, and wood in great aboundance, especially Cedar; and partly by reason the country is much subiect vnto earth-quakes, yet be there many goodly houses and stately pallaces of excellent workemanshippe and rare Architecture.

The people are more swarty of complexion then the Spaniardes be, almost like the tawny Mores, and something lesse of stature commonly then those of our nation be. They are for the most part of pregnant liuely witttes, of exceeding memory, of stoute couragious mindes, and wonderfull patience in occasions of aduersity. Commonly they be haughty and high minded, very desirous of

B 3   honour

honour and eſtimation. They do contemne all
other Nations in the world in compariſon of
themſelues, from whence proceedeth the
ſmall account they make of any ſtrangers that
come into theyr country. Pouerty doth not
with them diminiſh Nobility, nor Gentility
nor wealth gaine or increaſe it. The better
ſort do vſe great cerimonies of honour and
courteſy one towardes another: yea the common people as tradeſmen and artificers muſt
be vſed with reſpect, or elſe you ſhall obteyne
nothing at theyr handes: neyther will they
put vp iniury at any man without complete
reuenge. They are very carefull not to ſhew
feare or cowardize in any caſe: they ſtand
much vpon theyr grauity, and therefore they
carry thẽſelues alwaies very ſoberly & after a
ſtayed manner: in ſo much that it is held a
wondrous inciuility for any to make any
great noyſe, as ſhouting, hollowing, or the
like, whether it be in publike or priuate, at
home or abroad. To bring vp theyr children
to hardnes, as ſoone as they be new borne
they waſh them in ſome riuer, and when
they be weaned from the nurſe, they take
                                        them

them from theyr mothers, & bring them vp
most commonly in exercise of hunting & the
like : when they come to a certaine age they
change the forme & fashion of their apparrel,
vsing therein very many cerimonies.

They haue diuers fashions very different from ours : with vs men weare hattes
& women euer somethinge on theyr heades:
they both men and women go bareheaded at
all times, and in all occasions, both in the
heate and could, in sunne and wind, in
haile, in snow and raine : they mourne in
white as we do in blacke, & blacke with them
is worne in signe of ioy : we hould it good to
haue white teeth, they thinke it otherwise,
and therefore dye them black: we get on horse
blacke on the right side, they on the left : we
when in meeting we salute put of our hattes,
they put of theyr shoes. When they visit one
another, he that is visited must not go out
to meete the other that commeth to visit
him, nor rise vp if he be set in any place, but
rather contrary, if he be standing he sittes
downe to receiue him. Our manner of musicke
is not gratefull vnto them, our meates dis-

tastfull

taſtfull, our ſweet odoriferous ſmels odious and abominable. They cure their ſicke quite contrary to vs, giuing them raw meates, and ſalt and ſower thinges to eate. In ſteed of kniues and ſpoones they vſe two woodden ſtickes exceeding curiouſly, and after a farre neater faſhion then we they vſe to eate their meate. Whereas we write from one ſide of the paper to the other, they write from the toppe to the bottome of the leafe, making their lines downeward.

In all Iapone there is but one only language, the which yet is ſo exceeding copious, and of that variety, that it may ſeeme to be many, by reaſon that for almoſt euery thinge they haue very many wordes, whereof ſome do ſignify it when mention is made thereof in contemptible manner, others when in honorable faſhion; ſome are to be vſed onely by the common people, others only by thoſe of Nobility or Gentry: ſome are only for men, others only for women: theyr manner of writing is very different alſo from their ſpeach; and theyr writing letters from theyr writing bookes: theyr characters

characters or letters are of a fashion farre
different from ours, and of that nature that
with one only letter they signify sometimes
a whole word, sometimes many words.

   In times past there was but one only
King in all Iapone who was Monarch therof, and obeyed and reuerenced exceedingly
of all, and liued with wondrous state and
maiesty, and him they called the Dayri or
Vo, but these Dayries giuing themselues
at length by occasion of the great peace and
quietnesse they enioyed to sloth and idlenes,
and to all kind of voluptuous pleasures and
delightes, about 500 yeares ago were by
two principall captaines that rebelled against
them, dispossessed of a great part of the
Kingdome, they making themselues kinges
of all they could get and maintaine by force
of armes, and afterwardes others moued
by theyr example did the like: so that within
short time the Dayri, although he still remayned with the title of vniuersall Lord of
all Iapone, yet had he small or no iuris-
diction at all, only a power to giue titles of
honour and dignity according vnto mens
desires

defires or defertes, the which he enioyeth to thi day without any gouernement at all, fcarce hauing meanes to maintaine himfelfe in honorable fafhion.

Since thofe times to thefe, he hath euer beene accounted King our Emperor of Iapone that could by any meanes make himfelfe Lord of the Tenca *, that is, of fome few Kingdomes or Prouinces neere adioyning to* Meaco *, which is the principall Citty of all thofe countreys, as London is in ours; and fo in our dayes there haue leene three who haue had the name and āuthority of Emperour one after the other, not by any right or title of election or inheritance ; but obteyned by maine force, or other wrongfull meanes. The firft of them was called* Nobunanga *who conquered fix and thirty Kingdomes The fecond* Taycofama, *or* Quambacù, *who being a man very meanely borne, brought vnder his dominion fifty Kingdomes or Prouinces. The third is the* Xogun *who reygneth at the prefent, and hath rayfed the perfecution (whereof this booke intreateth) againft the Chriftians, and he as it feemeth* *ſeemeth is acknowledged as Lord of all the threeſcore and ſix Kingdomes of Iaponia.*

Theſe Emperours as abſolute Lords and owners of all the country, do diſpoſe of al thinges as their pleaſure, and therefore for their owne greater ſecurity as ſoone as they haue gotten the gouerment by force or other meanes into their handes, they deuide the kingdomes or prouinces vnto diuers of their freinds, with obligation that they ſhall ſerue them in time of war with a certaine number of men, at their owne charges and expences: and theſe againe do deuide their prouinces amongſt their freindes with the like obligation to be ready to ſerue them in all occaſions, reſeruing to themſelues ſufficient for the maintenance of their houſe and family: ſo that all the whole country doth in ſuch maner depend of the Emperour, that he giues and takes, rayſeth and pulleth downe, enricheth and impoueriſheth whome, and when, and how he pleaſeth. And it is the cuſtom amongſt them when they take from any one their Prouince or Eſtate, or change them to another, that

all

al the gentlemen and fouldiers that did depēd
vpon that perſon, do leaue that prouince to-
gither with him, and eitther go with him, or
elſe ſeeke meanes to liue in ſome other place,
the tradeſemen, artificers, husbandmen,
and laborers onely remaining therein.

Thoſe that be the Lords or petty kinges
of particular prouinces or kingdomes, as alſo
all other principall perſonages, as gouernors
of townes and Citties, beſides the obligation
aboue mentioned, are bound at the begining
of euery yere, betwixt the ninth & twentith
day of the firſt moone (for their acount is by
Moones, and after a different manner farre
from ours) to go vnto the Emperors Court to
do him homage, and acknowledge their obedience towards him, and togeather therwith
they muſt alwaies offer him ſome thinge of
good value by way of preſent, whereby he
draweth to himſelfe the greateſt part of all
the wealth of the contry, & by meanes thereof, togeather with his owne reuenews (which
amount to two milliōs or more euery yeare)
he groweth in ſhort time to be exceeding rich
potent, ſtrong, and ſo powerfull that none
almoſt

almost dare withstand or contradict him in
any thing, no though he make himself a God,
as diuers of them haue procured to be accounted and esteemed.

And indeed most of these that be a-
dored amongst them as Gods, were eyther
kinges famous for their valour in warre, and
feates of armes, or else Bonzos singularly
noted for their learning and eloquence, or
strict rigorous course of life. These last they
call Totoques, the other Camis, of whom
they aske only earthly goods, temporall blessings
and benefittes, as of the Totoques they do
onely the felicity of the future life. The principall or cheife of all these be two, the one named Xaca, the other Amida, whome they
worship and inuoke with great reuerence and
deuotion. Their Bonzos which be those that
teach and preach vnto them, as our preistes
to vs, be deuided into ten or eleuen diuers
Sectes, very contrary amongst themselues,
though the most of them do agree in denying
the prouidence of God, and immortality of
the soule, the which they do to the end they
may liue with more liberty, and more freely
giue

giue theſelues to al kind of lewd licentiousnes.
Beſides theſe Gods ſom do adore the Heauens
the Sunne and Stares, others Oxen, Stags and
other baſer creatures. Not farre from Meaco
they haue a ſumptuous Temple dedicated to
the Liſard, which they reuerence as the God
of learning, wiſdome and eloquence. Many
there be that do adore the Diuel who doth appeare vnto them in ſundry formes and like-
neſſes, and makes them confidently beleeue
that all thinges do depend of him, and that
they proſper or haue ill ſucceſſe according to
the deuotion they beare and ſhew to him.

     And in this miſerable blindnes was al
that whole contry vntil the yeare of our Lord
1549. in which the Bleſſed Father Francis
Xauier, a Preiſt of the Society of Ieſus, and
one of the ten Companions of the holy Father
Ignatius Loyola of happy memory, who was
the firſt Founder of that worthy Religious
Order, did enter thereinto to preach vnto
them the Goſpel of our Sauiour Ieſus Chriſt;
the which he did vpon this occaſion.

     There was in a certeine port towne
of Iapone called Cangoxima in the king-
                                    dome

dome of Saxuma *a wealthy substantial man*
named Angier, *who in his youth had com-*
mitted some enormous crime, and finding
afterwardes his conscience much burdened
and tormented therewith, used all meanes
possible he could inuent, or that the Bonzos
could imagine to aduise him, to obteyne some
remedy therefore, and procure the peace and
quiet of his mind: but hauing after experi-
ence made of all the remedies that any of the
Sectes of his country could affoard, found that
his affliction did still endure, he was euen al-
most out of hope of euer obteyning ease or
remedy; vntill it happening afterwardes that
the Portugalls *comming with some ships*
vnto Cangoxima *to traffique about mer-*
chandise, were an occasion of raysing a new
hope in him; for he falling into familiar ac-
quaintance with some of them, and after
much other talk hauing had by theyr meanes
some notice of Christian religion, as also of
the great Sanctity and holinesse of life of Fa-
ther Francis Xauier, *who at that time*
was famous in all the East Indies, thought
with himselfe, that perhaps by his meanes
he

he might find some salue for the soare of his
wounded and afflicted conscience : And ther-
upon resoluing to go and secke him out, he
left his house, wife and family, freinds kinsfolkes and country, and taking with him onely
a seruant or two he went with the Portugals,
& after many dangers past at sea of stormes,
tempestes, foule weather, and the like, he
arriued at length at Malaca, a towne of
great trade and traffique in the East Indies,
and there by good fortune to his great content he found the Father whom he sought,
and from thence went with him to Goa, the
chiefe Citty that the Portugalls possessed in
all those countryes: where hauing found by
following his direction as much ease and
comfort of his mind as he did wish for and
desire, and being sufficiently instructed in all
the mysteries of Christian Religion, he was
baptized by him, and named Pablo de la
santa Fè that is, Paul of the holy Faith.

　　Hauing thus obteyned his desire, and
being after some time to retourn againe into
his country, the Blessed Father Xauier,
whose whole desire was to propagate the
　　　　　　　　　　　　　　　fayth

fayth of Christ to the honor and glory of Almigty God, and for the saluation of mens soules, would needes accompany him, carrying with him other two of the Society, the one a Priest called Father Cosmo de Torres, the other a lay brother whose name was Iohn Fernandez both of them Spaniardes borne: and so they all departed from Goa in the moneth of April 1549. and at the end of May they came to Malaca, from whence they arriued at Cangoxima in Iapone about the middest of August: where being welcommed and well receiued of the freindes, kinred, and acquaintance of Paul the new conuerted Christian, and hauing with much labour and industry learned a little of the Iaponian language, they began to preach the Christian fayth publikely to all with the good leaue and liking of the Lord or Prince of the countrey, who hoping to haue some benefit by the comming of the Portugalls into his countrey was content to giue way to the Fathers, and let them preach: but afterwardes perceiuing that some of the Portugalls leauing his Porte went vnto a-

C   nother

nother not farre off called Tirando *in the Kingdome of* Tigen *, he withdrew his fauour from them , and by instigation of the* Bonzos *made a* Proclamation *, that vnder payne of death none of his subiects should leaue their former Sectes to imbrace the Christian religion . Whereupon* Father Xauier *after he had in vaine vsed all possible diligence to mollify the King, and suffered diuers incommodities and iniuries with exceeding patience , taking his leaue of those Christians that were already made , which amounted to the number of an hundred or there aboutes , he went vnto* Tirando *together with his two companions, where being now somewhat more expert in the* Iaponian *tongue then they were before , setting themselues to preach , partly thereby and partly by the rare example of their liues , they moued more in a few dayes to imbrace the fayth of* Christ *, and to receiue the holy Sacrament of baptisme , then they had done in a yeare before at* Cangoxima .

Father Xauier *did perswade himselfe that if he could get vnto* Meaco *, which was the*

the cheife Citty of Iapon, & the place where
the Cubosama, who was then the chiefe
King of all the country, did keepe his Court,
that there he might do more good, and sooner
come to giue notice of Christ and his religion
to the principall persons of the Kingdome,
then in any other place: and therefore hauing
commended the care of the new conuerted
Christians in Cangoxima to Paul the Iaponian, and those of Tirando to Father
Cosmo de Torres, he and brother Iohn
Fernandez tooke their iourney towardes
Meaco, and about the beginning of October
they got vnto Amanguchi a goodly Citty
at that time, for since it hath beene burned,
sacked, and destroyed, euen in the hart of all
Iapone, almost three hundred miles distant
from Tirando, whither being come, they
were carried vnto the king or Prince thereof, vnto whom they declared in the best
manner they could the principall mysteries of
Christian religion, he neither shewing liking
nor dislike of any thing they sayd: and afterwardes they did the like in the publike streets
and market places of the Citty, wherein by

C 2   reason

reason they were but meanely apparreled according to the custome of religious men, and spake the Iaponian language but very brokenly, they were not only derided and mocked of all, but also iniured and handled very hardly by some of the ruder sort. From thence they went vnto Meaco, and in their iourney which endured well nigh two monethes, they suffered exceeding many miseries. First they went barefoote all the way, and then because the wayes were very dangerous and full of theeues who murthered all they robbed, they were enforced to keep company with horsemen, to runne though the hard stony wayes, as fast as the others did ride, to wade also ouer many great riuers and other deepe waters in the way, hauing afterwardes no meanes almost to dry, rest, or ease themselues, no where finding any that would help or succour them, take pitty, or compassion on them, but many almost euery where that egregiously abused and iniured them: so that had they not carried some little rice in sachels on theyr backes for theyr sustenance, it is very likely they had perished

by

by the way for very want, and necessity.

Being now arriued at Meaco, *they found all the Citty in vprore and armes, no disposition at all for them to manifest the Christian fayth: whereupon they were enforced almost immediatly to retourne againe to* Amanguchi *the same way, and after the same fashion that they came from thence before. And there Father* Xauier *did resolue, notwithstanding all difficulties, to set and settle himselfe to the preaching and planting of religion: and because he had learned by experience that the* Iaponians *did neyther esteeme of men nor of theyr wordes, vnlesse they were in exterior good fashion, and well apparreled, therefore to accommodate himselfe vnto them for their greater good, he went vnto* Tirando, *and there at they charge of the king of* Portugall *he put himselfe in good apparell, and taking with him letters of fauour frō the viceroy of the Indies, and of the Bishop of* Goa, *which he had procured vnto the Princes of* Iapon, *and certaine small thinges brought out of* Europe, *as clockes, and such like curiosities,*

C 3 *the*

the which were giuen him by the Gouernor of Malaca *to bestow in such occasions, he returned backe againe to* Amanguchi *with Brother* Iohn Fernandez, *and two or three* Iaponians *in his company, where he made meanes to haue accesse vnto the King to whom by way of present he gaue those thinges which he had brought with him thither to that purpose. The king accepted of them willingly, and though he wondred at them as being rare and neuer seene before in those countryes, yet much more did he admire at the greatnes of the giuers minde, who did refuse a great quantity of gold and siluer, and other thinges which he offered him in requitall thereof, and only required that he would giue him licence to preach the fayth of* Christ *to whome, and where he would : the which he graunted easily, and assigned him besides a certaine house of good capacity, where he and his companions might re-mayne.*

This licence being thus obteyned, the which was all the holy Father did desire, he and the Brother his Companion did set themselues

themselues immediatly to worke, preaching
all the day time in the streetes and middest
of the market place, an innumerable number
of people flocking about them, some to see
and heare what they sayd, others to laugh at
their manner of speach, others to marke
their actions and mocke at their behauiour:
and in the night they did the same in the
house where they lodged to those that came
thither to visit them, as many did, some
of courtesy but most of curiosity And in this
manner they spent diuers monethes without
seing any fruit at all of all their labours
vntill at length one was conuerted vpon this
occasion. Brother Iohn Fernandez preaching one day in the street according to his
wonted manner a Iaponian that passed by
in a scornefull manner, did spit at him;
and the filthy fleame falling iust vpon his
face, he wiping it of, without making any
shew of the least impatience in the world,
with great serenity of mind went forward in
his speach: the which being well marked and
obserued by one of the standers by, caused
him within himselfe to frame this conceipt:

C 4   doubt.lesse

doubtlesse this doctrine must needs be very good that causeth in the professors thereof so great humility patience and constancy of mind, in suffering iniuries and indignities: and thereupon the Sermon being ended, he followed the brother to their house, where hauing learned the Creed, the ten Commaundementes, our Lords prayer, the Salutation of our B. Lady, and diuers other prayers, and being sufficiently instructed in all the mysteries of Christian religion, and sorry for the sinnes of his former life, he was the first in all that Citty that did receiue the holy Sacrament of baptisme, and thereby was made a member of Christs holy Church and Congregation. Soone after him diuers others also were baptized, and within a short tyme the number of Christians there amounted to fiue hundred or there abouts, and all of them (as they well shewed in many occasions that happened afterwardes) exceeding constant, vertuous, and perseuerant.

Matters being come to this good passe, letters were brought vnto Father Xauier, in which wa signified that it was precisely

cise'y necessary for him to returne in person
to the Indies vpon vrgent busines : leauing
therefore behind him Father Cosmo de
Torres, and Brother Iohn Fernandez to
conserue and increase the best they could that
little flocke of Christ, which he had there
begunne and gathered, he went backe to Malaca, and afterwardes to Goa, from whence
he sent some more of the Society vnto them
to help towards the conuersion of Iapone:
the which they and others that succeded them
did with such diligent care and industry (God
Almighty blessing their labours & concuring
thereunto with many miracles wrought by
them) that within the space of twenty yeares
or thereaboutes, there were in that country
by their meanes and good endeauors more
then an hundred and forty thousand Christians, and amongst them many persons of great
worth & estimation, as the King of Bungo
a very potent Prince, who for the deuotion
and veneration he bare to Father Francis
Xauier, when he was baptized, which was
some yeares after the holy Fat'ers death,
would neede, be called Francis by his name.

The

The King of Arima *also named* Don Protasio, *and his brother* Don Bartholomew *Prince of* Omura, *a most pious and valerous Gentleman*, *and diuers other Noble men*; *who all agreeing amongst themselues to the end the whole world might vnderstand how sincerely they did beleeue and imbrace the fayth of Christ, in the yeare* 1583. *they sent from thence to* Rome, *which is well neere ten thousand miles, foure young Gentlemen, some of them very neere of kinred vnto the kinges before named, to render obedience in their names vnto the most pious Pope* Gregory *the thirteenth, who then liued, as vnto the vicar of our Blessed Sauiour here on earth and cheife head & pastor of all the Christians in the world*.

After Father Xauier *his death, which was in the yeare* 1552 *the Superiors of the Society of* IESVS *still continued sending some of their subiectes to* Iapone, *to procure the increase of Christianity therein, and some yeares ago others of other holy Religious Orders, as of* S. Dominicke, S. Frauncis *and* S. Augustine, *haue gone thither also*

to

to the same in'ent, whereby their holy endeauours many thousandes of soules haue beene
deliuered out of the darknes of superstition
and Idolatry, and brought vnto the light of
Christes onely true and Catholike Religion.
And in such prosperous manner did they go
on assisted by the help of God, and all of them
in concord of hart, and vnity of faith, that
there was no smal hope that the whol country
would within a short time haue beene eyther
all or the most part thereof conuerted to the
Christian faith, vntill now of late the rai-
sing of the persecution (whereof this ensuing
relation doth intreat) hath been a great hin-
derance and impediment thereunto, as you wil
easily perceiue by perusing thereof, from the
which I will now no longer detayne you.

THE

THE
FIRST PART

OF THE RELATION
OF
THE PERSECVTION
RAYSED IN THE
YEARE OF OVR LORD,
M.DC.XIIII.

Againſt the Chriſtians of Iaponia.

Wherein all the Prieſts and Religious perſons
were baniſhed thence, togeather with diuers
other Chriſtian *Iaponians* : with the Martyrdome of ſome for their conſtant perſeue-
rance in the profeſſion of their Fayth.

---

*Of the beginning , cauſes , and occaſion
of the Perſecution.*

CHAP. I.

T HE Church and Chriſtiany
of *Iapon* which now 66. years
agoe was firſt founded by
the Bleſſed Father *Frauncis
Xauier* of the Society of Ieſus (and euer
ſince then hath beeue principally con-
ſerued

serued next after God by the labours and
good endeauours of the Fathers of the
fanie Society) hath fuffered many great
and greeuous perfecutions, euen as the
Primitiue Church did in the firft beginning thereof . Some of thefe Perfecutions haue been particuler only in fome
Countries or Prouinces fubie&t to certeine Lordes or petty Kinges: and thefe
haue beene fo many and fo continuall,
that fcarce euer the Chriftians haue
beene without fome moleftation in one
part or other , as may appeare by the hi-
ftory of that Country written at large
by Father *Luis de Guzman* of the Society
of IESVS . Others haue been generall ,
caufed by the Lords of the *Tenca* , who
were the Monarchs of al *Iapone*, not only
banifhinge the Fathers of the Society ,
deftroying their Churches and houfes ,
and taking away from them all that they
had , but alfo banifhing likewife the
Chriftians of the country, together with
their kinred, freinds, and familiars, con-
fifcating their landes and goods , and
finally

finally bereauing the alſo of their liues.

2. But neuer hitherto hath any beene
eyther ſo generall, or ſo rigorous, as
that which *Minamoto Iyeyaſu*, who at
this preſent is the *Xogun* or *Cuboſama*,
King and Lord of al *Iapon*, did raiſe now
two yeares agoe in the yeare 1614.
For that if heretofore the Fathers were
baniſhed out of ſome one country or
prouince they ſtill found refuge in ſome
other part or place of the kingdome: and
although *Taycoſama* the predeceſſor in
gouerment to him that now reigneth did
twiſe caſt downe and deſtroy all their
Churches, and commaunded them to
depart his kingdome; yet alwayes had
they a Church ſtandinge on foote in
Nangaſaqui (a port towne in *Iapon*) for
the vſe of the Portugall merchants who
traffique thither; and vnder colour of
that, they not onely remained there, but
alſo from thece went ſecretly into many
other prouinces of the kingdome, and
did great good amongſt the Chriſtians;
who likewiſe were neuer before vſed ſo
hardly

hardly as at this time they be . For that
the *Xogun* in this persecution hath not
onely caused all the Churches to be burned and razed to the ground , and giuen
expresse charge that no Priest nor preacher of the Christian religion whether
he be a stranger or free-denizen should
remaine therein , but also hath cōmaun-
ded, that all the Christians do leaue their
faith and religion vnder paine of banishment out of the kingdom , or being put
after many torments to some cruel kind
of death . Vpon this occasion there haue
happened many accidents worthy of
memory , to the great honor and glory
of Almighty God, and very like to those
of the primitiue Church , as in the discourse of this Relation wil appeare.

3 . The causes and reasons of this so
rigorous sentence and proceeding of the
Xogun ; and of the execution thereof, be
diuers , some of old , and some of new .
Of old is the hatred of the Diuell , who
hauing had peaceable possession more
then a 1000. yeares of al that kingdome,
and

and seing that now of late by reason of
the preaching, teaching, holy life and instruction of the Fathers, many thousands
of soules were daily drawne from Idolatry and superstition to the knowledge
and seruice of the true and euerliuing
God , their onely Lord, maker, creator,
and redeemer , and that very probably
within smal time if they were permitted he should be altogether dispossessed
of the tyrannical dominiō he had so long
exercised vpon them, did therefore al his
endeauours to hinder their prosperous
proceedings ; especially for that already
(besides many thousandes that were
departed this world) there were then
liuing more then two hundred and fifty
thousand Christians, so zealous & feruorous in the seruice of their Lord and Sauiour , that besides their diligence to
learne and know all the duties of good
Christians , and their care in keeping &
obseruing gods precepts and comman-
dements , many of them did animate
themselues to attaine to a higher perfe-

D   ction,

ction, and to follow the Euangelicall Counsailes of Virginity, Chastity, voluntary pouerty, recollection and religious life.

4.   This I say made him bestir himself, and moue the *Bonzos* his Ministers, to hate the Fathers bitterly, and to procure their disgrace by al means possible: the which was not very had to do, because themselues did see that their credits with the people was much decreased since their comming into the country, as also their gaines greatly diminished. For which cause within short time after the entráce of the Fathers, to auert the minds of the people from them, they published that they were Diuels in humane shape sent from hell to hinder the happy successe of the *Iaponian* Sectes; that the kingdomes wheresoeuer they entred went presently to wracke; that they did eate mans flesh, and the like. But all these reportes being found out in short time to be wholy false and vntrue, reproachfull flaunders, and forged calumniations, they

they changed their note and begun another tune, protesting in their Sermons
that it ought not to be endured, that a
few poore straungers (as the Fathers
were) should be permitted to procure
with so great diligence & endeauour as
they did, the destruction of their Idols,
Temples and Sectes, that had beene alwaies so highly esteemed of all their
ancestours; and to bringe into their
country another new law and religion,
and customes wholy opposite and contrary vnto those which so long time had
beene professed and practised therein:
complayning moreouer, that those that
were made Christians in many thinges
were more obedient vnto the Fathers
then vnto their owne Princes & naturall
Lordes, and that for their religion they
would by their perswasion loose both
their liuinges, honors, and their liues.
Moreouer they sayd, that it was not pro-
bable, nor possible, but that the Fathers
vnder colour of preaching the religion
and faith of Christ, had some pretence
D 2

of

of matter of ftate: nor that any wife man
could perfwade himfelfe, that men of
iudgment and difcretion (as the Fathers
feemed to them to be) would euer come
from fo far countries, with fo great coft
and charges, through fo many and fo
euident perills and dangers, both by fea
and land as they did, only for the faluation of the foules of other men, as they
pretend to do, efpecially of fuch as they
neuer fawe before, nor do any wayes
belonge or apperteine vnto them : and
that therefore doubtles there was fome
other temporal refpect that moued them
thereunto.

5. And to giue a greater colour of
likelyhood and fhew of reafon for what
they did affirme, they added thereunto
diuers thinges which were moft true, as
that the Spaniardes (of which Nation
moft of the Fathers be) be very warlike
people, and how they haue conquered
the Eaft and Weft *Indies*, the *Ilandes* of
Molucas, and the *Philippines*; that all the
Chriftians conuerted by the Fathers are
very

very obedient vnto them , ready to do in
all thinges what they shall aduise , and
that they are al very much vnited among
themselues .

6 . With these and the like reasons
they easily persuaded diuers Princes of
the Country , who commonly are very
iealous of their states, to haue the Fathers
in suspition, seing especially before their
eyes what a reuolution had beene made
a little before in their owne country by a
Bonzo of *Ozaca* , who vnder colour of
defending certaine Sectes , had troubled
& molested both *Taycosama* , *Nobunanga* ,
and al the princes of *Iapon* . Many of these
reasons were alledged by *Taycosama* both
in the yeare 1587 . when he first banished
the Fathers, as also when he renewed the
persecution in the yeare 1596 . wherein
he made exceeding hauocke among the
Christians. For although he were moued
thereunto principally by reason of the
desire he had to haue taken the great
Spanish galeon , called *S . Philip* , which
passed by that way vnto *Noua Espana*
from

from the *Philipines* ; yet was he also not a
little prouoked by the foolish wordes of
a certaine Pilot, who being asked how
the Spaniardes had gained so many kingdomes, he answered that they went first
to traffique into them, and that if therein
they eyther receyued iniury of any, or
were not wel vsed, or not receiued by the
people of the cõtry, that then they made
warre against them, and ouercomming
them, tooke possession of their kingdom
and estats. And being asked if they did
not also for that cause send religious men
before them, he answered, yes : the
which, although it were most false and
fabulous, yet did *Taycosama* take it as a
sufficient occasion to rayse a cruell persecution against al the Christians of
Iapone.

7 .   This suspition was confirmed in
them, yea & much increased by certeine
Englishmen, and *Hollanders*, who in the
time of this *Xogun* do not onely traffique
but also some of them reside and dwel
within *Iapone* : for they partly through
the

the hate they haue and beare to religious
men and Catholikes, and partly for feare
least the Spaniardes should be a meanes
to hinder their traffique thither , haue
made many malicious and most vile reportes , euen the very worst they could
imagine or inuent , both of the one and
other . As for example that the religious
men are dangerous persons, both wicked
and rebellious : that they do not preach
Chrifts true Religion , but onely their
owne fancies & imaginations , and that
for that caufe they haue beene ofttimes
banished by Christian princes in *Europe*
out of their kingdomes and dominions ;
that the Spaniardes haue no other end
nor intention in comming thither , but
onely to bereaue them of their kingdom
and gouerment , alledging to that purpose , and as it were in proofe thereof
many particuler examples to make some
shew of truth .

8 . That they were the authors of
these falfe reportes , came to be knowne
from the *Xogun* himfelfe, who one day in

D 4   speach

speach vsed these wordes : That if the
Kinges and Princes of *Europe* do banish
the Fathers out of their countries, I shall
do them no iniury to send them out of
mine. These and such like malitious ru-
mors and reportes were in themselues
sufficient to haue beene causes of greater
harmes and mischeifes then they were
for a longe time, had not Almighty God
in a maner bound and held the Gentiles
handes, who with the desire of continu-
inge traffique with the *Spaniardes* and
Portugalls, eyther would not heare, or
when they heard would neuer giue credit vnto such wicked and malitious vn-
truthes.

9. The Diuell perceiuing this, and
knowinge well how that by occasion of
the traffique from the *Indies* and *Macan*,
Christian religion found first entrance
into *Iapone*, and how by meanes thereof
it hath hitherto also beene there conser-
ued, and that if it should cease, religion
could not probably be of longe continuance there, he did therefore his vtmost
endeauour

endeauour to hinder it, and for that cause
it is most likely, that first of all he moued
the Heretikes to go thither, to the end
that by their false reportes they might
bring into discredit with the Gentiles the
Catholike religion : and offer to bring
them the same merchandise that the *Spaniardes*
and *Portugals* haue done hitherto.
Secondly, that the *Xogun*, through the
false informations of a Gouernor called
Safioyedono, and other his adherentes
should most iniustly commaund that the
ship of traffique of *Macan* should be set
vpon, and taken most iniuriously, the
which in the yeare 1610. by that occasió
was set on fire and burnt to the domage
of diuers Christians, and little lesse in
all then a million of losse.

10. And finally that some *Iaponians*
did wrongfully take and vsurpe at the
same time, almost all the goodes of the
ship called *S . Frauncis* of the *Philippines*
which did ariue at the port towne of
Quanto, where they offered so many and
so grosse iniuries vnto the *Spaniardes* and
Portugals

Portugals as were scarce to be endured: and matters came thereby to that passe, that it was thought it would haue been an occasion of the total ruine and destruction of all the Christianity of *Iapone*, had it not pleased Almighty God by the good endeauours, diligence and intercession of some freinds, and especially of *Don Iohn Arimadono*, who at that time was in great fauour with the *Xogun*, to haue pacified matters, and so calmed the tempest that was then rising against them.

Of the beginning of the Perfecution in the Prouince of Arima.

CHAP. II.

DON *Iohn Arimadono* aforesaid was Lord and Prince of all the Prouince of *Arima*. He was an Auncient Christian, a great benefactor, and as it were the very prop and piller of the whole Church of *Iapone*, as well for that he had caused the conuersion of all his subiectes to the Christian faith, by

meanes

meanes of the Fathers of the Society,
whome he alwaies fauored very much,
not onely permitting them to preach
freely to all in his dominions, but also
giuing them succour & harbour therein
euen in the time of the greatest fury of
Taycosama his persecution, exposing himselfe thereby to the danger of loosing his
honour, estate, and life, and that not once
but oftentimes, although he were therefore much molested both by some freinds
of his owne, as also by the Lords of the
Tenca.

2. There was close by his country
of *Arima* aother Prouince which indeed
of right belonged vuto him, and had
beene sometime possessed by his ance-
stors, but now was vsurped by another
man. This prouince *Don Iohn* did much
desire to obtaine by meanes and fauour
of the *Xogun*, & to that end he vsed some
meanes not so conformable either to reason, or to the law of God as might haue
beene wished and desired. One was to
marry his sonne & heire, who was already

dy married to another wife, vnto a
yong lady that was grandchild to the
Xogun. Another was in hauing a hand
by the appointment of the *Xogun* in the
burning of the ſhip of *Macan*, whereof
we ſpake before, vnder pretence of certaine iniuries done vnto ſome *Iaponians*,
it being indeed nothing ſo, but onely a
deuiſe and deceit of *Saſioyedono*.

3. It ſeemed vnto him that by making the people of that prouince which
he pretended Chriſtians, by deſtroying
Idolatry in it, and building Churches
to God therein, that theſe ſinnes which
he committed, to condeſcend with the
Xogun & get his fauor, would be therby
wel ſatisfied, and the ſcandal giuen vnto
the Chriſtians eyther wholy taken away
or elſe much qualefied : but it happened
much otherwiſe (and indeed thinges
though they be good and holy, if they be
brought to paſſe and compaſſed by euill
meanes, can haue no good end, and
commonly haue bad ſucceſſe.) For firſt
of all Almighty God permitted him to be
deluded

deluded by a false fellow , a counterfait
and feigned Christian called *Dayfachy*
Paulo, who receauing of him many bribs
both for himselfe and for other fauorites
of the *Xogun* , did persuade him that the
Xogun had made him a graunt of that
Prouince , and that the Letters patentes
therof were already drawne , but afterwards it was found out all to be a meere
cosenage and decept. Wherupon *Dayfachy*
was put in prison for it , and being conuinced of Forgery , was condemned to
death , and finally burned for fallisiyng
the Kinges Letters . Then *Don Iohn* his
owne sonne called *Saiemon Nosuque* , by
the perswafion of his new maried wife
the grandchild of the *Xogun* , and also
carried away with ambition and desire
of comaund , ioyning and vniting himselfe with some of his Fathers mortall
enemies , made such complaintes , and
framed such articles against him vpon
this occasion , that they caused him to be
banished by the *Xogun* , and his estate to
be assigned to his sonne . And finally by
procurement

procurement of his owne sayd sonne, &
his wife whom he had caused to marry
against all right and reason, hoping by
her meanes more easily to compasse his
desires, to honor and strengthen his house
and family : by their meanes, I say, and
others, who feared least comming to
answere for himselfe he would discouer
their false dealinges, and accusations
layd against him, he was at length depriued of his life. And in this ended the
vnlawfull and euill grounded worldly
pollicy of *Don Iohn*, although he dyed
very penitent for that he had done, with
great signes of true sorrow and contri-
tion for his sinnes, and of good preparation for his death, forgiuing al iniuries
had beene offered him, and asking pardon of all whome he had offended. And
in him the whole new planted Church
of all *Iapone* did loose exceeding much,
for he, as I said before, was a great de-
fender, supporter, and a stay thereof.

4 .   By reason of the bad procedings
of *Don Iohn* in the thinges aforementi-
oned,

oned , and his euill succeste therein , the
Gentills tooke occasion to speake their
pleasure of the Catholike religion , and
to calumniate it as though the sinnes and
imperfections of some particuler persons
that professe it , were to be imputed to
their faith , it being in it selfe most per-
fect , pure , and holy . The *Xogun* also
thereupon begun the persecution of the
Christians of the Prouince of *Arima* ,
who were all *Don Iohn* his subiectes , and
most louing towards him . For being as
he was euen from the very begining of
his gouerment so great an enemy to
Christian religion , that he commanded
that none of his house should be Christians vnder paine of loosing both their liuinges and their liues , protesting publikely that all the princes of *Iapone* should
do the like with their subiectes , and earnestly entreating *Don Iohn* oftentimes
that he would renounce his religion , as
being vnworthy to be professed of so
principall a person as he was , and that
he would permit Temples to be built to
the

the Idols in his Countryes; vpon this
occasion of the banishment of *Don Iohn*
he sent word vnto his sone *Sayemon
Nosuque*, that seing he did him the fauour to place him in his Fathers estate
and gouernement, as also to admit him
to marry with his owne Grandchild,
that in recompence thereof he would
haue him leaue to be a Christian, and
not only himselfe, but all his seruantes
and subiectes also, and that he should
banish the Fathers out of his Countryes.
And for the execution thereof he sent
vnto him for his director and chiefe
counsayler in the businesse *Safioye* the Gouernor of *Nangasaqui* a great enemy to
Christians. *Sayemon* durst do no other
then obey him in all he commaunded,
for feare of loosing his estate, and so
hereupon immediatly through the counsayle of his new *Herodias*, his pretended
wife, and the policies of *Safioyedono*, he
begunne the persecution of *Arima*, and
of that was occasioned afterwardes the
generall persecution in all *Iapon*, as after
                                    shall

shall appeare.

5. The *Xogun* moreouer did commaund enquiry to be made amongst his
owne Seruantes, Souldiers, and Captaines, to see if any of them were Christians; and hauing found that fourteene
of them were so, all of them persons of
note and quality, and fiue or six of them
noble, rich, and his great fauorites, he
was exceedingly offended therewith:
and hauing vnderstood that after diligence vsed with them, there was no
meanes to make them change their
mindes, he banished them all togeather
with their wiues and families, in such
rigorous manner, that he commaunded
all the Princes of *Iapone* vnder greiuous
paynes and punishmentes, that none
should giue them any succour or enter-
tainment whatsoeuer.

6. Great was the courage and constancy which these good Christians
shewed in this extremity in loosing their
landes & liuinges for our Sauiours sake,
rather then they would leaue his holy
fayth

fayth whereof they made profession, being ready also to loose their liues for the same cause, if occasion had beene offered. They suffered exceeding much, themselues, their wiues, and children wandring vp and downe, and going secretly here and there, not finding any place where to abide. *Iulia* also a principall Lady of the Court who was banished for the same cause to a little Iland scarce inhabited, did suffer there exceeding much in this occasion.

7. Many noble personages in the Courtes of *Yendo* and *Suruga* did imitate the *Xoguns* proceedinges in this kind, but aboue all the Prince of *Toxogun* did shew himselfe most cruell and rigorous, moued partly by the *Xoguns* example, but principally incited by the wordes of an English Pilot who spake most bitterly against religious men and Spaniardes, making their persons odious vnto him, and all that they did suspitious. Whereupon many Christians of great worth & quality were sent into banishment. And
this

this affliction had beene much more
greeuous and more generall , had not
Itacuradono the Gouernor of *Meaco* , an
honorable, moderate and morall man, &
a friend vnto the Fathers, ſignified vnto
the *Xogun* , that it was no reaſon that all
the Chriſtians, being as they are, people
that liue in the Kingdome well and quietly , and do hurt and iniury to none ,
ſhould be puniſhed for the fault of ſome
one , or a few particuler perſons of their
Religion : neyther do I hold it (ſayd he)
for good policy , now that the Kingdome is in peace and quietnes, to ſtrike a
ſtring that may make to great a noyſe, &
perhaps put matters more out of tune ,
then is by vs imagined .

8 . Vpon this good aduiſe the *Xogun*
did for a while ſomewhat temper himſelfe , and gaue licenſe againe that the
Fathers of the Society might remaine ,
and haue one Church within the Citty
of *Meaco* : and thereupon , and by reaſon
that the Gouernour did cōmaund to proclaime that the *Xoguns* former order was
E 2   not

not to be vnderstood of merchantes,
tradesmen, or common people, but only
of Souldiers and Gentlemen, many of
their Churches did remaine vntouched,
and the Christians in some good quietnesse, for that many other Princes
winked at them, as at the Fathers also. So
that this persecution first of all begunne
as it seemeth in *Suruga* and *Yendo*, although the principall blow did fal vpon
the prouince of *Taccacu*, or *Arima*, which
is all one.

9. For when notice was giuen in
the Country of *Arima*, with what determination the new *Arimadono* was
comming from the Court, great was
the griefe and affliction generally of all
the Christians thereof, but aboue all
vnto the good Fathers of the Society the
newes was most heauy, seeing the euident danger of those whome with so
great paynes, care, labour and trauaile
they had conuerted to the Christian
fayth, and for so many yeares instructed
therein: and that the Churches which
                                    with

with so great costes and charges they
had builded for the seruing and honoring of Almighty God, should now eyther be destroyed, or els turned into
Temples of Idols for the seruice of the
Diuell. And finally that, that flocke of
Christ whereof they had had so great
care, should be now deliuered to the
custody of cruell wolues the *Bonzos*,
without hauing any Pastor that might
feed it, keepe it, and defend it. Like
good sheepheardes therefore they be-
ganne to animate their sheep, and arme
them by meanes of the holy Sacramentes, which they ministred vnto
them, making also many spirituall exhortations vnto them and pyous sermons, perswading them therein to
patience, constancy and perseuerance,
to fasting, prayer, and true penance for
their sinnes.

10.   As soone as *Arimadono* was arriued at *Ximauara* which is the first towne
of that Prouince, together with *Safioye*
and another fauourite of the *Xogun*, who
E 3   were

were his wicked counsaylers, which
was vpon the ninth of Iuly, they published an edict or Proclamation, in which
was commaunded that all his subiectes
and seruantes should leaue the faith of
Christ, and send for the *Bonzos* to instruct them in the sectes of *Iapone*, ap-
pointing withal three Iudges vnto, whō
they gaue order to procure by all meanes
possible, that all the Gentlemen of quality that had any rentes, reuenewes or
pensions from the *Xogun*, should immediatly leaue to be Christians vnder paine
of loosing both them, and the rest of
their goods and liuinges, and thereby be
reduced to extreme pouerty and most
miserable estate. And vpon the 13 day
of the same moneth he sent word vnto
the Fathers of the Society, that seeing the
Xogun had forbidden the profession of
Christian religion, his pleasure was they
should immediatly depart out of his
Country, leauing their Churches and
houses as they stood. The ornaments of
the Church, the pictures, and their bokes
they

they had caused before to be conuaied to
Nangasaqui , and so they difpatched now
the fooner obeying to his commaund ,
though not without great greife and
affliction , for they had in that country
a Colledge the beft and biggeft in all
Iapone , a Seminary alfo where they did
bring vp many yong youthes and children of the *Iaponians* , teaching them learning and vertue , latin , muficke , and
the characters of the Religions and fectes
of *Iapone* , and the manner how to con-
fute them , which hath beene one of the
beft and moft efficacious meanes for the
conuerfion of thefe Gentiles. They had
alfo in that Country of *Arima* fix other
places of ordinary refidéce , befids other
Churches and houfes , which now and
then they vifited to the number of three
fcore and ten : and all thefe in one day
were confifcated , and they caft out of
them . Some of the Fathers remayned in
the contry fecretly & difguifed , together
with fome of the Brothers alfo & youths
of the Seminary , for the better helping

of

of the poore afflicted Christians thereof.
And although they did it not without
great labour and paines, and exceeding
danger of their liues; yet was it wel re-
compenſed with the great good they did
thereby among the Christians, who
with great care, loue, and charity did
hide them, keep them, and maintaine
them.

11.   The Iudges appointed by young
Arimadono for the examining and proceeding against the Christians, ſent for
ſome of them one after another, and did
their beſt endeauors to perſwade them
to do ſome exterior act whereby at leaſt
they might make ſhew to haue obeyed
to the *Xoguns* commaund in leauing of
their faith. Some although very few did
eaſily condeſcend to their requeſts, ho-
pinge thereby to gaine the fauour of
their Prince; and theſe all of them were
ſuch as eyther were not well grounded
in their faith, or elſe were men of euil
life, and bad corrupted conſciences.
Others moued and ouercome with the
entreaties,

entreaties, importunities, and teares of
of their kinred, freinds & acquaintaine,
shewed some weaknes and fraylty at the
first, it seeming to them eyther no sinne
at all, or else not very great exteriorly to
dissemble for a time, so that inwardly
in their hartes they did not leaue their
fayth, thereby to giue contentment to
their Prince, and saue their owne estates.
But being afterwards aduised of their
fault, and told how great a sinne it was,
they were so seriously sorrowful and penitent therefore, and did recompense
their fall with so great courage, feruour
and constancy, that some of them afterwards endured most cruel martyrdome,
and others suffered incredible afflictions
want, misery, and pouerty for their faith
after they had publikely reuoked that
which before they had of frailty done:
and this they did before the Iudges, and
Aximadono himselfe, asking pardon
of all for the offence and scandall they
had committed through feare, and in a
manner vnawares. All the rest answered

E 5   so

fo couragioufly and conftantly, that they not only remayned conquerors, but alfo fo confounded the Iudges, that they durft not paffe any further in examining and queftioning them: and in this occafion there happened many thinges very notable and worthy of memory, not only of men and women, but of younge Virgins alfo and tender children, which would be to long & tedious to rehearfe.

12. *Thomas Ondafeibioye* a principall and moft valerous fouldier, and one of the beft Chriftians of that country, who had two feuerall times before been banifhed for his fayth, once in the yeare 1587. with *Don Iufto Veondono*, whofe fubiect then he was, and the fecond time in the yeare 1602. loofing then likewife all the liuing that he had for the fame occafion, was one of the firft that was called by the Iudges: but he not going in perfon vnto them vpon fome occafion, fent them his anfwere in writing in this manner following: *Neyther I, nor my brother* Matthias; *nor any perfon of my*

houfe

house shall shew himselfe disloyall to Almighty God, nor deny the holy *Religion* in the which from children we haue byn brought vp, nor will we change our mindes for all that the world can offer or affoard. I and my brother, my mother, my wife and children are ready to do any thing that Arimadono shall commaund vs, so that it be not against the law of God, and holy fayth which we professe. Presently as soone as he had sent this message, he sent for a Father of the Society, of whome they all receiued the holy Sacramentes, thereby the better to prepare themselues to Martyrdome : and although at that time it did not take effect, yet afterwardes it did, as shall appeare in the sequele of this Narration. Many others did answere to the Iudges with like constancy and resolution ; the which being perceiued by *Arimadono*, because he was loath to loose so many true & trusty faythfull and noble Captaines, he therefore dissembled the matter at that time with *Thomas* and diuers others, giuing them secretly leaue to be Christians
stians

ſtians ſo that exteriourly they made no
great ſhew thereof : but they were
all reſolued, and he certified, that they
would not make any ſhew of the contrary in preiudice of their conſcience &
religion .

*Of ſome that were baniſhed, and others put
to death for the fayth of Chriſt in the
Prouince of* Arima.

CHAP. III.

ARIMADONO fearing he
might diſguſt the *Xogun*, and ſo
perhaps looſe his Eſtate, if he
did ſhew himſelfe remiſſe in perſecuting
the Chriſtians (although on the other
ſide he ſaw the courage they ſhewed)
commaunded vpon the twentith day of
Iune, that the landes and goodes of fiue
rich Gentlemen ſhould be confiſcated,
and that they, their wiues, children, and
families ſhould be put out of their houſes,
taking no other thinge with them, but
only

only the apparrell on their backes: char-
ging withall that none should intertaine
them in their houses , nor giue them any
food , reliefe , or suftenance vnder payne
of seuere and grieuous punishment . He
caused moreouer officers to be set in the
high wayes , port townes , and paffages
to the end they should not escape out of
his country, but perish there for hunger,
want , and misery , euen in they eyes of
their dearest friendes and kinsfolkes .
Much they suffered by this meanes for
diuers dayes , liuing only vpon hearbes
and such wild fruites as they found growing in the woodes , being perpetually
expoſed to the cold , the wind and raine
which at that time happened to be very
much , vntill at length the Christians of
Arima , and other places found meanes
to help and succour them , and by the
order and direction of one of the Society they made themſelues little cabbins
of straw , among the mountaines for
their aboad , therein ſpending their time
in faſting , prayer , and reading of good

and

and holy bookes, and so they led their
liues a great while, not only with great
patience, but with much ioy also, comfort and content.

2. *Arimadono* perceiuing by this
that what hitherto he had done against
the Christians did little or nothing preuaile, he resolued with himselfe to put
to death some of them, to wit, such as
had shewed themselues more forward
and feruorous : by which meanes the
happy lot of martyrdome befel vnto two
brethren the one called *Michael Soday* of
fifty yeares old or therabouts, the other
Matthias Coychi of one and thirty. They
were both of them borne in a towne of
that Prouince called *Ariye*, their parentes
were persons of good quality and very
worthy Christians. *Michael* was alwayes
accounted very deuout & feruorous, &
from his very childhood he was of so
great vertue, purity and integrity, that
none euer noted in him any thing that
might be a mortall sinne. He was but
weake and sickly, by reason of the hard
vsage

víage of his body with fasting, hayre-
cloth, disciplines, and other penances.
All his delight was in hearing sermons,
and reading good and pious bookes, in
somuch that he seemed rather a religious
man then secular. He was very chari-
table and desirous alwayes to help others
all he could, for which cause he was generally beloued of all, and respected and
esteemed as a father. By the appointment
of the Fathers of the Society he had for
the space of fifteene yeares the care and
direction of thirteene Congregations or
Confraternities into which the deuouter
sort of Christians for their excercise of
vertue had put and placed themselues.
And in this imployment did his brother
Matthias help him, being as like vnto
him in good qualities and vertuous in-
clination, as he was in bloud and natural
condition. When the Fathers were banished from *Arima* (as before is mentioned) *Michael* called togeather all the
Prefectes and Officers of the thirteene
Congregations, and told them that the
time

time was now come in which they muſt
all ſhew their faith, and the deſire they
had of the ſaluation of their ſoules : Let
euery one therefore (ſayd he) aske thoſe
of his Confraternity what diſpoſition
and courage they feele and find within
themſelues. Whereupon amongſt themſelues they made a catalogue or role, in
which within ſhort time more then fifteene hundred with great ſpirit and reſolution did write their names in ſigne
that they were ready & prepared to giue
their liues and ſuffer al kind of torments,
rather then leaue and forſake the Chriſtian religion.

3.   *Michael*, and his brother were
the two firſt whoſe names were written
in the Catalogue, and he ſavd, he did
deſire it ſhould be ſo, becauſe he hoped
by that meanes he might animate
others to do the like . And the reaſon
why he wiſhed the reſt would imitate
him and his brother therein, was to the
end, that if the Iudges ſhould offer any
more to call the Chriſtians to examination,

tion, seeing their names written in the
catalogue they should haue no cause to
doubt of their resolution & conformity
in desire to dye for Christ. They had a
Father of the Society hidden amongst
them, who with great care and secresy
went from one place to another, sayd
masse, preached & administred the holy
Sacraments vnto them. But the diuell
not being able to endure that those two
good brethren should do so good seruice
vnto God, nor that the Christians should
liue with such loue & feruor as they did,
did so dispose that *Arimadono* and his
Iudges came to haue notice and intelligence of all that passed : which being
knowne to them; and they easily perceauing that whilest those two holy brethren liued, they should not be able to
do any thinge with the Christians of
Ariye, they therefore condemned them
to death, comitting the execution therof vnto two principall men whome they
willed to do it secretly, because the
Xvgun had not commaunded that they

should

should put to death any of the Christians but onely that they should moleste them in such manner, that they of their owne accord for the auoiding of those troubles should leaue their Fayth and Religion.

4. Vpon the Eue of *S. Iames* of the yeare 1612. the Father of the Society went to *Michels* house, and there sayd masse the two dayes following, heard their confessions, gaue them the Blessed Sacrament, and then retourned to a little Cottage where he did lye hidden. In the afternoone, which was vpon the day of the glorious Saint *S. Anne*, did God Almighty choose to crowne these two happy brethren with the crowne of martyrdome. *Michael* was taken and carried to a place where sometimes had stood a Church of the *Misericordia*; and for that those that were to execute the Sentence were his friendes they notifyed it vnto him, and wished him to prepare himselfe to dye. Presently he lifted vp his eyes and handes to heauen giuing

firſt

firſt thankes vnto Almighty God for ſo
great a benefit, and afterwardes he ſayd
vnto thoſe that brought him the newes :
This is a fauour which a long time I haue
deſired at God Almighty his handes, and
being ſo weake and ſickly as I am, it ſeemed
to me that I ſhould haue dyed of ſome ordina-
ry ſickneſſe and diſeaſe, and therefore now I
am exceedingly reioyced with ſuch happy
newes and ſo glorious a lotte · Then he
kneeled downe vpon the ground and
prayed a little ſpace when as the executioner came to him and ſayd, Brother
Michael I beſeech you, that ſeing you are
to dye for the loue of God, that you
would intreate him to pardon me this
ſinne, for I am alſo a Chriſtiã & do this
office God knowes of force and much a-
gainſt my will. He anſwered with great
mildneſſe, that he would do it very willingly, and ſo his head was preſently
ſtroken of whileſt he was inuoking the
holy name of Ieſus. His Brother *Matthias*
they tooke at the ſame time in his owne
houſe, as he was foulding vp the orna-
F 2 mentes,

mentes, which the Father that day had
vſed in the holy Sacrifice of the maſſe,
and carrying him aſide, they gaue him
three or foure woundes, with which he
fell downe and dyed, ſaying with a loud
voyce, *Ieſus, Maria*.

5. The executioner that cut of *Michaels* head did great reuerence to their
two holy bodyes, and taking ſome of
their holy reliques, he gaue notice to
the Chriſtians of their death and cauſe
thereof. So many came thither to reuerence theyr bodies, and to get ſome of
their reliques, that they could ſcarce get
them buried all that night: at length they
buried them, though afterwardes they
were taken vp againe and carried to the
Church of *Nangaſaqui*, where they
were likewiſe much reuerenced of all,
ſome taking peeces of their apparrell
ſome parcels of their hayre, others ſome
of their bloud: many therewith made
the ſigne of the croſſe on their own fore-
heades deſiring much to imitate and follow them in dying for their fayth. An
old

old man of threescore and ten yeares
called *Ioachim*, as soone as he had notice
of their death, went running to the
place where their bodies lay, and imbra-
cing *Matthias* his body by the feete, he
most earnestly desired the executioners
who yet remayned there, that they
would do the like to him, seing he also
was a Christian, and had promised *Mi-*
chael to dye in his company.

6. Some monethes before this matter happened, *Lucy* the mother to these
two holy martirs, a very deuout and vertuous Christian, did see in a vision a
most beautifull child, who hauing two
pretious stones in his handes, shewed
them vnto her, and she desiring to take
them in her handes, he vanished away.
The next day following he did appeare
againe with two nosegayes made of
many goodly followers, and when she
desired to haue taken them as before, he
vanished away againe: likewise the third
day he appeared againe with two beautifull red roses in his handes, at which
she

she wondring, told her sonne *Michael*
of it, and he afterwardes related it to
another brother of his who is of the
Society: not long after she dyed, and it
seemes that Almighty God thereby
would let her vnderstand how gratefull
and beautifull the soules of her two
sonnes were in his heauenly eyes.

7. The same sentence of death was
executed vpon *Leon Quita Quinzaye-
mon*, on the two and twenty day of August 1612. He was a Gentleman of a
good house, and a very valerous souldier
of fifty yeares of age or thereaboutes :
he was borne at a towne called *Chinxina*,
and from his youth very vertuous and of
exemplar life. When *Arimadono* came
first to *Ximauara*, *Leon* sent him word
that if he meant to make vse of his seruice, it could not be but vpon condition
that he would giue him leaue to liue a
Christian, for that otherwise he would
not serue him. He went vp and downe
two monethes and more without his
sword, expecting an answere from
Arimadono,

Arimadono, animating with great feruor all to conftancy , and to that end vifiting the neighbour townes and villages . And fome wondring to fee him go without his fword , he told them : *Seing that I am not to defend myfelfe when they come to kill me for Chriftes caufe , I haue no need at all to weare my weapon.* Going vp and downe in this manner he, found that the Chriftians of one towne durft not bury publikely one that was dead ; and reprehending them for their cowardize therein , they told him they feared fome hurt and domage would befall him for the great boldneffe which he fhewed . To which he anfwered : *What can they do to me more then kill me, and for that I am very ready whenfoeuer they will , for there is nothing that I more defire then to dy for Chrift*: and faying fo , with his owne handes he buryed the dead body of the Chriftian .

8 . The Iudges did procure by all meanes poffible to perfwade him to accommodate himfelfe vnto the time, and
F 4

fo

fo he might enioy his liuing and be in
fauour with his Prince : and a certaine
Noble man that loued him very well,
called *Camon*, who was Vncle to *Ari-*
madono, after diuers perfwafions fayd
vnto him : What matter is it man, if
our Prince will go to hell, let vs make no
moreado but go with him thither too.
To whom he anfwered : *My Lord the*
obligation which the feruant hath to his mai-
ster, and the fubiect to his Prince doth end
togeather with this life, for in the next life
they haue no power nor authority at all: and
if your Lordfhippe will not beleeue me make
tryall if you pleafe., and call any of thofe cap-
taines that haue dyed in your feruice, or in
the feruice of your anceftors, and fee if they
do now anfwere to your call. In fuch thinges
therefore that doe concerne this prefent life, I
will very willingly ferue my Prince, but in
thofe that do pertaine vnto the next and
whereon my faluation doth depend, he muft
pardon me, I cannot nor I will not do it. And
vnto a brotherinlaw of *Arimadono* that
did intreate him concerning the fame
matter

matter he anſwered ; *Although I conf ſſe*
it will be ſomething difficult vnto me to ſerue
now one that hath left to be a Chriſtian , I
hauing before ſerued in the warre two ſo good
Chriſtian Princes , as were Don Iohn and his
brother Don Stephen , yet notwithſtanding
obtaine you that I may liue freely in my reli-
gion , and I will do willingly that which you
deſire me . In many other occaſions likewiſe he ſufficiently ſhewed his great zeal
and feruor which for breuities ſake I do
not heere rehearſe .

9. In concluſion *Arimadono,*becauſe
with his example and ſpeaches he did
much animate the reſt, gaue com maund
vnto two ſtróg ſouldiers that they ſhould
kil him ſecretly , for the reaſon before ex-
preſſed . They therefore ſent for him one
day vnto the caſtle , and he imagining
the cauſe to be that which indeed it was,
went thither with great alacrity ; and the
ſouldiers going out to meet him, asked
him whither he wét ? He aſwered that he
went to the Caſtle called by the Prince :
wherfor ſaid they? to haue my head out of

sayd he , becaufe I will not leaue to be a
Chriftian : and in this manner they wēt
talking with him , and he wifhed them
they would haue care to looke to the faluation of their foules, all other bufineffes
whatfoeuer in comparifon thereof being
of fmall account and confequence . He
made the figne of the Croffe vpon himfelfe many times as he went alonge the
way , & comming to a place where there
had beene a Church of the Society , he
kneeled downe vpon the ground , and
prayed for a while : which done he ri-
fing vp and going forward in the way
one of the fouldiers with his fword gaue
him fo great a blow vpon one of his
fhoulders , that he cut him downe into
the breft : he then pronouncing the holy
name of *Iefus* three times aloud , vnbuc-
kled his rapier, and cafting it away from
him did his endeauour to bleffe himfelfe
with making the figne of the Croffe, and
fo fell downe and dyed . The Chriftians
came thither prefently , and becaufe the
fentence that *Arimadono* had giuen a-
gainft

gainst him was publikely knowne, as also the cause thereof, togeather with the disposicion and preparacion he made for martyrdome, they therefore tooke his holy body, and sent it secretly to the house of the Society of Iesus in *Nangosaqui*, where it was buryed with all due respect and reuerence.

10. The happy deathes of the three foresayd martyrs caused so great feruour and courage in all the Christians of that Country and Estate, that now they did not thinke nor talke of any other thing, but onely how to prepare themselues to imitate and follow them : to that end by the counsaile and aduise of one of the Society, they began in the Citty of *Arima* to renew their Confraternities, not admitting into them any one, but onely such as were fully resolued to giue their liues, and all they had, yea and to suffer all kind of tormentes rather then to deny the faith of Christ. They made amongst themselues certaine lawes and rules, and set downe the fastes, the disciplines,

plines and other pennanes they were to do. Then they did deuide themselues into *Decuria's* (Companies of ten) to the end that meeting so in diuers places they might the better help one another . And the like was done by the Christians in al the townes of that whole country of *Arima* with a kind of holy emulation : but before any one could be admitted into any Confraternity , they did many pennances and other thinges of piety to dispose themselues thereto . The like was done by the women, and by the children also ; the womē thinking that in matters of deuotion they ought not to be inferior vnto men , and the children desiring and endeauoring to imitate theyr parentes piety .

11.   And this was the preparation which the cōmon people made, although they were not comprehended in the Proclamation : and we may with reason thinke that , that which the gentlemen and others of better sort did make , was not inferior vnto this . Those who , as I sayd

sayd before, at the entreaty and importunity of their freindes had in the beginning exteriously condescended to do some thinges not so conuenient, being now exceeding sory and repentant for their fault, desired no other thinge so much, as some good occasion wherein publikely to acknowledge their error, & to make profession of their faith. For which causes it being a custome among the *Bonzos* in their festiual dayes, in signe that one is of their sect, to take a booke made by *Xaca*, which is called *Poquequio*, and to put it vpon the heads of their parishioners or sectaries, saying therwithall a certaine prayer: and one of them hauing intreated *Arimadono* that vpon a certaine solemne day, he and his Courtiers would do this ceremony, they conspired amongst themselues not onely not to do it, but also to disgrace the *Bonzo* if he did persist therein. The day appointed came, but notice being had of their determination, and both *Arimadono*, and the *Bonzo* being afrayd, that if the ceremony

mony were done, it would redound more
to their disgrace and to the encoragemēt
of the Christians, they thought it therefore more conuenient to omit the ceremony, and so it was done, *Arimadono*
himselfe alone going to visit the *Bonzo*
without any more ado. Wherewith the
Gentlemen were not a little grieued because they had lost that good occasion of
publishing their mindes, which yet they
determined to manifest, and did that
very day, going all together vnto the
Iudges, vnto whom they spake in this
manner : *We be all Christians, and are wil-*
ling and desirous to suffer banishment, and
death rather then forsake our fayth and re-
ligion : and seeing that we haue not had
meanes to signify so much to Arimadono in
publike, we desire you to do it for vs. So many
they were that went thither with that
protestation, that although *Arimadono*
were so much offended therewith that
he commaunded they should be all put
to death, yet could it not be put in execution, vnlesse he would haue left himselfe

selfe without seruantes to attend vpon him, or at least beene depriued of the more and better sort of them.

12. One among the rest named *Leon* hauing shewed himselfe so constant that he was condemned to death therefore by *Arimadono's* speciall order, because he vnderstood that a friend of his thinking to doe him a pleasure had counterfayted his hande, and going to the Iudges therewith, assured them therby that he had reuolted from his fayth, he tooke foure witnesses with him & went vnto the Iudges, telling them he was a Christian, and that the subscription which had beene shewed vnto them as his, was not his, but counterfayte and false. The Iudges hauing heard him, gaue order he should be sent immediatly into banishment. His wife thinking that for this action of her husband both he and she should haue beene put to death, put on the best apparell she had, expecting therein the sentence and execution: but as soone as she vnderstood that the punishment

nishment of death was changed into banishment, leauing of her gay attire, and
her husband laying aside his weapons, &
loosing all his wealth, they departed
from their house in poore apparell, desirous to loose and leaue much more then
they had done, for our Blessed Sauiours
sake.

13. *Arimadono* at the beginning of
the first moneth of the yeare 1613. went
vnto the Court according to the custome
of *Iapone* to visit the *Xogun* for that new
yeare, and being on the way his Iudges
wrote vnto him of the great feruor of
the Christians, and how that euery day
some came before them to make potesta-
tion of their fayth: and therefore they
desired him he would consider what they
ought to do therein. He answered that
for a warning and example to the rest
they should thrust out of *Arima Don Iohn
Tacuyn*, who was his owne great Vncle,
a graue and aged Gentlemen of great
esteeme, and a father to the Christians,
taking from him the greatest part of his
                              reuenewes.

reuenewes. And that they should depriue *George Tsfengi* (who was a very worthy Chriftian , and had beene a famous Captaine about *Meaco* , and banished alfo from the kingdome of *Fingo*, & loft his caftle for his confciencefake)of al his liuing , & banish him out of the country of *Arima* , & finally that they should put to death *Thomas Onda Feibioye* togeather with his brother mother and children .

14. This *Thomas* was he that an-fwered the Iudges fo refolutly as we re-lated in the end of the precedent Chap-ter: and *Arimadono* becaufe he was a man of notable courage and valour had giuen him once leaue to liue a Chriftian, but not many monethes afterward he be-gun againe to intreate and vrge him very much that he would accommodate himfelfe vnto the time , affuring him that therein he should giue him great content: Whereto he anfwered , that neyther in honefty nor Chriftianity he could, nor would shew himfelfe difloyall vnto God : but yet for all that he ftill

G   perfifted ,

persisted, vrging him euen till a little before his departure towardes the Court,
and was much grieued to see he could
not preuaile against his constant resolution; the which Thomas wel perceyuing,
grew more carefull of himselfe : and to
be in better disposition for whatsoeuer
might succeed, he made a generall confession of all his life vnto the Father that
went secretly and disguised amongst
them, of whome alwayes when he came
to his house to celebrate the holy sacrifice of the masse, he receiued the Sacramentes with particuler deuotion: and all
his discourse with him commonly was
what a happy thing it was to giue ones
life for the loue of God. He vsually did
much pennance, and gaue himselfe to
prayer, grieuing oftentimes that he had
lost so many good occasions to dye for
Christes holy fayth, and true religion.

15.   Vpon the 21. of Ianuary one of
Arimadono his Gouernors sent for him to
his house, and another of them sent for
his brother *Matthias*, and there secretly
                                    they

they caused them to be slayne, cutting
of both their heades, they calling at that
time, vpon our Blessed Sauiour with
great deuotion and content, commen-
ding their soules into his holy handes.
Thomas was one and forty yeares old
when he was put to death, and his brother *Matthias* was one and thirty, both
of them very well beloued of all sortes of
people, for their good nature and rare
qualities, but much more for their vertu
and Christianity. The Iudges sent word
forthwith vnto their mother *Martha* of
the death of her two somes, signifying
withall that shee and her grandchildren
must beare them company. The which
newes although to some it might seeme
heauy, yet did shee receiue it with signes
of great ioy and contentment, and as
though it had beene a message sent from
heauen vnto her: and giuing thankes to
Almighty God, & to those that brought
it her, shee sent immediatly for her two
grandchildren whose names were *Iustus*
and *Iames*, the one of eleuen, the other of
nine

nine yeares old. Their mother *Iusta* was pardoned her life at the intreaty and intercession of some of her kinsfolkes, although she nothing at all desired it, it being to her worse then death not to dy in that occasion.

16. When her children tooke their last leaue of her, they spake these wordes vnto her : *God be with you deare Mother, for we be sent for to accompany our Father vnto heauen ; both he and we will expect you there.* She kissing and blessing them, gaue them great charge they should not be afraid of death, nor shew any signe of feare or cowardize at all. Then she and her good mother-in-law took their leaue of one another with many teares, ech giuing the other good counsaile and aduise : which being done, the two little children with their good grand-mother were carried to a place by the sea side which was appointed for their execució; whither being come, *Iames* the yonger of the two remembring the good counsaile that his mother had giuen him, did himselfe

selfe vncouer his owne necke and layd downe his little head vpon the blocke in readines for the hangman to cut it of, & then deuoutly saying *Iesus Maria* three seuerall times the Executioner bereaued him of his life. His brother *Iustus* with like constancy and more then manly fortitude did follow him. Then their holy Grandmother *Martha* a graue matrone of three score yeares and one, and the example of al that country of *Arima*, glad to haue seene the Sacrifice of her sonnes and grandchildren for so good a cause, deteyned her selfe a good while in her prayers, and then giuing to some present certaine holy reliques which she had about her, and to others her beades which she wore about her necke, and some part also of her apparrell, she desired them al very earnestly to pray for her to Almighty God, and so falling againe to her prayers she had her head cut of by the same executioner that before had beheaded her two grandchildren. Her head together with her bloud was carefully

taken

taken vp by the Christians that were
there present, notwithstanding the presence of the officers, who eyther durst
not or would not contradict their deuotion therein. Afterwardes both hers, as
also the bodies of the children were
carried to *Nangasaqui*, and there buried
withal respect conuenient, in the Church
of the Fathers of the Socyety of Iesus.
The sentence pronunced against *Don
Iohn Tacuyen, Arimadono* his great Vncle,
as also against the worthy Captaine
George Yesengi of banishment and losse
of their goodes whereof I spake before,
was also with all rigour put in execution.

Of eight Christian Iaponians that were bur-
ned aliue for the faith of Christ.

CHAP. IIII.

SAFIOTE, seeing that with his
violent manner of proceeding,
putting some to death and banishing others, he was so far from obteyning
of

of his purpose and desire, that rather
matters were worse now then they were
before: for those that were but somwhat
bold before, were now much more encouraged by the examples they had seen,
and with the hope of victory & heauenly reward, and those that had shewed
some weaknes & frailty at the first by the
same examples were moued to be very
sory and repentant for their fall, and
rose vp againe with couragious resolution: he now determined to change
his rigour into another kind of crafty
cunning persecution. He sought out
therefore a certaine *Bonzo,* an auncient
preacher of the *Iaponian* Sectes, that
was very famous in the Courtes of *Suruga* and *Yendo,* and brought him to *A-
rimadono,* telling him that if he could get
the Christianes of his country to heare
his Sermons, without all doubt they
would very quickly little esteeme,
wholy giue ouer, and leaue the Christian
Fayth. He wished him therefore to carry
him to *Arima* with him, and to make

G4   him

him preach therein . *Arimadono* to giue
content vnto *Safioyedono* and the *Xogun* ,
was very willing therewithall, and *Ban-*
zui (for ſo was the *Bonzo* his name) was
not backward but rather exceeding glad
to go , thinking doubtleſſe he ſhould do
ſome great exploite and gaine immortall
Fame in conuincing and conuerting of
the Chriſtians : the *Bonzos* of *Meaco*
who by experience knew of how ſmall
effect their Sermons are againſt the Chriſtian Fayth, in the meane tyme langhing
in their ſleues to thinke how wholy his
hopes would be fruſtrated.

    2 .   Aſſoone as the Chriſtianes of
Arima had intelligence of the *Bonzo* his
comming towards them , they begane
forthwith to prepare themſelues: And
ſent vnto the Biſhop and vnto Father
Prouinciall of the Society , to know of
them what they might do, neyther to preiudice their Conſciences, nor to be wanting in their duty to their Prince. And
it was reſolued that they ſhould neyther
go out to meet the *Bonzo*, nor afterwards

                     to

to visit him . The which although some
of them did not obserue , going at the
petition of the chiefe Gouernour to visit
him , yet when they went they carried
their beades in their handes , and *Agnus
Deies* at their neckes , in signe that they
were Christians .

3 .   It was appointed by *Arimadono*
that there should be a Temple or Chappell, and an Altar made for the *Bonzo* his
vse : and because the Christians neyther
for loue nor money , neyther by threats
nor intreaties could be brought to put
their hands thereunto , they were forced
to fetch from other places Carpenters &
other workmen who were Gentills , for
the framing & making thereof . When
the Temple was finished and all in readines , *Banzui* would needs now haue
them come to heare him preach . Some
went of curiosity to heare what he
would say, but before the end of his Sermon they did so laugh , so mocke and
deride him both in the Temple and after
in the streets, that the poore *Bonzo* almost

G 5   besides

besides himselfe did grieuously complaine to *Safioye* , that insteed of honouring him as he expectedthey had brought him thither , as it seemed , wholy do disgrace him , and make him loose his credit : Telling him withall , that if *Arimadono* would shew some exemplar punishment vpon some of the principall Christians, the rest would be terrified therewith . Whereupon the matter was proposed to *Arimadono* , and by him , and them it was determined , that eight or ten of them should be put to death publikely, togeather with their wiues and Children .

4. Great was the feruour that was at that tyme amonge the Christians, continnall their prayer and frequent their doing of penances .Inmany places they made the prayer of Forty houres continually without intermission , carefully following the counsailes, direction and exhortation of the Fathers of the Society , that in disguised habits liued amongst them. Innumerable daily entred

into

into the Confraternities , writing their names in the Cataloges, euen with their owne bloud which to that end they let out of their bodies , and making protestation, that affisted by the grace of God, they would remaine firme and constant in the confession of their Faith. As soone as it was knowne that some of them should be put to tormentes , and afterwardes to death , a wondrous great ioy arose amongst them all, ech one congratulating the good newes with his neighbour, freinds, and kinred; euery one also desirning that it might be his happy lot to be one of those that should dy for the Christian Cause in that occasion .

5 . Out of all the townes of the country there was six or seauen of euery Confraternity sent to the Citty of *Arima* to giue Intelligence when , and where the sentence should be put in Execution before mentioned , with intention all of them to be present there to make publike protestation of their faith , and to shew how desirous they were to dy therefore. And

And this was in such manner that almost al tradsmen and artificers did leaue their worke and occupations , and merchantes did suspend their traffique vntil they saw what would be the yssue and conclusion thereof .

6. But *Safioye* hauing vnderstood of all that passed amongst them, fearing some vprore, and doubting that he should be blamed for it at the Court : seeing also that their resolution was such , that to vse rigor towards them, should be but to cast oyle into the fier, rather augment their constancy then otherwise, he comanded no more should be done in that busines : and thereupon the Christians returned all vnto their houses with intention there to prepare theselues against another tyme for Martyrdome . Notwithstanding this command, of *Safioye* , *Banzni* the *Bonzo* at the petitiõ of *Arimadono* his wife , who was an eager enemie vnto the Christians, would needes vrge some Gentlewomen and pages that wayted in the pallace, to take of him certaine

scroles

scroles and graines which the *Bonzos* vfe
to giue, and which they call *Iuzus*, and
Maburi; but it was his misfortune and
hard hap to gaine as little honor in this
matter as he had done before by his Sermons; for fome of the yonger fort vpon
that occafion not only refufed to take
his *Iuzus* with deuotion, but alfo made
him and them an obiect of their myrth;
and fome of them being to much vrged
by him in that bufines caft his trumperie
in his face, for which he did reueng himfelfe euen to the full, caufing fome of
of them to be put in prifon for it, and
others to be banifhed.

   7. A little after this, there came
newes from the Court, that by occafion
of a little Chappell that was built by the
Chriftians, for certaine poore leprous
perfons of *Yendo*, the *Xogun* was fo much
offended therewith, that after many
examinations and other diligences vfed
he comanded and caufed 28. of them to
be put to death at three feuerall tymes,
they all fuffering moft conftantly fo glo.
                                    rious

rious a Martyrdome because they would
not deny the Fayth of Christ . Eight of
them were put to death vpon the 16 .
day of August , and fourteene vpon the
17 . the rest in the next moneth following . Moreouer he comanded that all the
Christians , whose names were written
downe in the Catalogue (whereof vpon
some other occasion perhaps heereafter
we may speake) should be compelled to
leaue their fayth. This newes made great
impression in *Safioyedono*, and thereupon
he tooke occasion to cause the Martyrdome of those whereof I purpose now to
speake to be put io execution . *Safioyedono*
when he departed from *Nangasaqui* vnto
the Court at *Suruga* , sent word to *Arimadono*, that it was reported in the Court
that he was a Christian , and that therefore he did not only not endeauour
that his subiects should be otherwise ,
but rather procured that the faith
of Christ should daily florish more
and more in his dominions : and that
doubtlesse the *Xogun* now at his going to
the

the Court would aske him how the matter stood, and that he must needs certify
the truth although much againsthis wil,
which being knowne , it seemed to him
very likely that he would besharply rebuked for permitting matters to be in that
manner that they were . He wished him
therefor as a freind to consider wel what
he did, by reason he perceaued that his
Estate vpon this respect was in great hazard and ieopardy .

8.   With this message *Arimadono* was
at his wits end and almost besides himselfe , seeing that it seemed to him he
had already done almost all he could a-
gainst the Christians , and for that cause
had depriued himselfe , by putting some
to death and sending others into banishment,of the best , most faithfull and ancient seruants of his house . And thinking with himselfe that he should be vtterly vndone , if *Safioye* did make such a
Relation to the *Xogun* of him as he sayd
he would , he publickly protested , that
he had now no Christians in his house
and

and that he therfore wondred very much
any such reportes should be made of him.
When he made this protestation he imagined that none would haue contradi-
cted that which he had sayd, and so therby he should sufficiently haue complyed
with *Safioye* . But some that thinking
perhapps, that they had obligation in
that occasion to manifest themselues,
answered him aloud and sayd; yea, and
if it please your Excellency there be máy
Christians in your house and those also
that are very desirous to spend their
bloud for their fayth and religion : and
there withall eight Gentlemen of the best
note and quality in al *Arima* did manifest
themselues for Christians .

9 .   *Arimadono* was now much more
greeued and afflicted then before , and
caused *Safioye* his letter to be shewed
them , desiring them for the loue they
bare vnto him , that they would accommodate themselues vnto the tyme. They
answered him with couragious resolution , that in no case, and for no respect
they

they could condeſcend to his requeſt
therein . The day following which was
vpon the firſt of October he called them
all vnto him , one by one and very ear-
neſtly , teares accompaning his wordes ,
ſpake vnto them in this manner . My
eſtate and honor wholy ſtandeth at this
preſent in your handes :for as you cannot
chooſe but know I haue many enemies
who by this meanes do ſeeke my vtter
ouerthrowe. For the loue therefore that
you beare me, I beſeech you make but
only ſome kind of ſhew before the *Bonzo*
for one day , nay but for one houres
ſpace that you be no Chriſtians , and afterwards do euen as you pleaſe . To the
reſt of the Chriſtians you ſhall do a great
good turne in doing ſo , for I with this
will reſt ſatiſſied and trouble no one man
more , and if you do it not I ſhall be compelled to proceed with rigor againſt the
all . And although perhaps it be a ſinne ,
you are not ignorant that *S . Peter* being
an Apoſtle , yea the Chiefe of them al! ,
denied Chriſt , and yet afterwards ob-
H teyned

teyned pardon for it : much more may
you who do not deny him in your hartes
nor yet for feare , but only make a shew
to deny him , and that for a very little
tyme , to conserue thereby a whole Prouince and the Christians therof in peace
and quietnes .

10.   With these reasons and the like ,
fiue of the eight did yeald themselues
vnto his will , and afterwardes he gaue
assault vnto the other three , reducing to
their memory the many benefits they
had receaued of his house and family : he
told them he meant to do them more ,
and that it was no reason for a thing that
might so easily be remedied to put in hazard his honor and estate . But they answered him with such couragious constancy , grounded vpon solide and substantiall reasons , that being out of hope
to bring them to his becke , he went presently to *Nangasaqui* to take his leaue of
Safioye, to tell him what he had done, and
take his further aduise what afterwardes
to do .

11.

11 . The three glorious Confessors of Christ returned very ioyfully home , confessed themselues immediatly with one of the Society , and procured to prepare themselues for martyrdome which now it seemed they were almost assured of . And vpon the fifth day of October came the sentence from *Nangasaqui,* that they their wiues and Children should be burned aliue . The same day in the afternoone it was notified vnto them , and a certaine house appointed them for their prison , vnto the which they went most willingly without any officer or other person to carry or conduct them thither. The names of those that went in this maner were these, *Adrian Tacafati Mondo* and *Ioanna* his wife, *Leon Fayaxida Lugutyemon* and his wife *Martha* , with two children , *Iames* of eleauen yeares of age and *Magdalen* of eighteene , a very vertuous virgin , who with the licence of her ghostly Father and good liking of her parentes had made a vow of her virginity some yeares before , *Leon Taquendomi*

H 2 *Canyemon*

Canyemon, and *Paul Canyemon* his sonne.

12.   And togeather with these did two other valorous souldiers of Christ enter into the prison to beare them company in dying for their fayth, although afterwards they were put out from thence with no small griefe vnto their hartes, because their names were not in the Catalogue. Only there was wanting *Monica* the wife of *Leon Taquendomi*, with a daughter of hers of nyne yeares old. The reason of their absence was, because it was reported credibly to her that the women should not be put to death, whereupon she and her daughter not without many teares had before taken their leaues of her husband and sóne, and they of them: but afterwardes *Leon* vnderstanding the truth, he vsed meanes to giue her notice thereof, which when she knew, presently leauing her house, her goodes, and all she had, she came with her daughter running after him, but she was stayed in the way, and caried by force vnto the house of an ancient

cient Gentleman Vncle vnto *Arima-*
dono , who becauſe he had brought her
vp of a child , would needes ſaue her and
her daughter from the fyer . And although they were both of them much
afflicted therewith , and vſed many intreaties , that they might be ſent vnto
the priſon with the reſt , yet could they
not by any meanes obteine it . For
which cauſe *Monica* that night leaped
ouer a wall and ſo got out of the houſe
to go vnto the priſon , but being found
by the watch , ſhe was hindred & caried
backe againe.

13. Of thoſe fiue which yealded to
the intreaty of *Arimadono* , as I ſaid before , foure of them falling ſoone after
into conſideration with themſelues ,
were exceeding ſory for their fault , and
vſed all meanes poſſible to amend the
ſame . Firſt therefore , they ſought out
a Father of the Society with whom they
did confeſſe their ſinnes ; after their confeſſion , they made a Catalogue of the
rentes and goodes they had , the which
they

they gaue vnto the Gouernors, saying
that they from their childhood had been
Christians, and how being seduced by
the intreaties of their Lord, they had shewed frailty only for one day, for the
which they were exceeding sorrowfull,
and did repent themselues, and so deli-
uering vnto them their goodes, they
went vnto the prison, and would haue
entred in, but were not permitted by
the Officers. Agreeing therefore among
themselues they went all togeather into
a house thereby, and from thence they
wrote a letter to the *Bonzo Banzui*, in
which they did protest how they were
Christians, and did desire to dye for
Christ, and that the frailty they had shewed proceeded of deceipt, and that they
were very sory for it. *Arimadono* returning from *Nangasaqui* & hauing knowledge of their repentance, commanded
they should be set free, and that they
might liue Christians. But they with
wondrous griefe and sorrow not to haue
obteyned their desire, causing their heads

to

to be al ſhauen, in token that they meant
to forſake the world , leauing theire
houſes, goodes, and liuinges, did volun-
tarily baniſh themſelues , to expect ſome
other where a better occaſiō to ſuffer for
their fayth .

14.   As ſoone as the ſentence was
knowne and publiſhed that the three a-
boue named with their wiues and children ſhould be burned , there was ſo
great a concourſe of Chriſtiās to ſee that
ſpectacle from all the townes and villages therabout , that all the wayes and
ſtreets were filled with men and women
of all ages , ſortes , and qualities : and
which is worthy to be noted amongſt
them all , they being more then twenty
thouſand in number , there was not ſo
much as one only ſword or other weapon whatſoeuer, it being an vſual thing
there for almoſt euery one to go with his
weapons ; but inſteed thereof euery one
had their roſary or beades in their hands
to pray vpon, and nothing els ; and many
of them came in ſuch haſt , that they for-

got their very meate, leauing alfo their
houfes open, and not one to keepe them
or looke vnto them. *Banzui* the *Bonzo*
for very feare retired himfelfe into the
caftle, and a certaine difciple of his went
in all haft to *Nangafaqui*, and there reported that the Chriftians were vp in
rebellion, and that they had killed his
Maifter. *Safioye* was much troubled
with this newes, but the Gouernors did
affure him that there was none there
that had any Armes, and that they did
not fo much as offer to make the leaft re-
fiftance in the world. In fo much that it
being told them, that *Arimadono* had comaunded they fhould be driuen from
thence with mufket fhot, there was not
one that fled, or ftirred, but with great
filence and deuotion there they ftood all
that night praying on their beades,
which euery one held in his handes,
fetting forth fo many lights in euery
place, that the citty of *Arima* feemed to
be another ftarry firmament.

15.   So great was the ioy of the holy
prifoners

prisoners and the thankes they gaue
vnto Almighty God to see themselues in
that estate, that they could scarce con-
teine themselues through the great content they felt. That night they spent all
in prayer, disciplining themselues also
all of them togeather. It was imagined
most conuenient by some in authority,
that they should be put to death secretly,
and their bodies to be hidden, partly for
feare some violence would be offered by
the Christians, and partly because their
Reliques should not be reuerenced. But
the Prefectes or Stewardes of the Confraternities hearing thereof, came vnto
them and did assure both them and al the
officers there should be no disorder at all
committed, and desiring them that sup-
posing they would not let them be companions to the other in their Martyrdoe,
yet at least they might accompany them
vnto their death, the which was grāted,
And so presently they caused to be made
vpon the Sea shore, a mile or thereaboutes from the Castle, a little house

H 5   with

with eight pillars of wood, putting in the midest therof and round about many boughes, and straw, and dry canes: and to the end none might come neere the said house they made a great pale round about it.

16. The day following, which was vpon the 7. of October, the Gouernors did signify vnto the designed Martyrs that, that very day the sentence should be put in execution: and therwith their ioyes were much increased, they giuing thousandes of thankes vnto Almighty God for so great a benefit. Those of the Confraternity casting themselues down before their feet, did congratulate their great happines, and desired something of them for a relique and memory: But they in al humble manner answered they feared they should not bee worthy of so great a good, intreating them to pray to God for their perseuerance: particulerly *Iames* the little child of nyne yeares old, when any came to him to congratulate his happy lot, that he should be

a

a martyr of Chriſt , he would run away
from them ſaying: *I am not yet a Martyr.*
Me thinkes I ſee the crowne and do deſire it
much, but as yet I haue it not , and therefore
it is yet to ſoone to giue me that honour and
that name . They all of them put on their
beſt apparel therin to go vnto their Martyrdome , and ouer them they had long
white garments like to ſurplices ſuch as
thoſe of the Confraternity of *Cochinot-*
zu did ordinarily vſe in their ſolemne
feaſtes .

17 . Now all of them being ready ,
thoſe of the Confraternity to accōpany
them vnto the place of execution framed
a proceſſion , and ſuch a one as the like
perhapps was neuer ſeene before : For
that in the middeſt of a Nation and coū-
try of Gentills and Infidells , there went
more them twenty thouſand Chriſtians
euery one with his beades in his hands ,
all deſirous to be partaker of the Martyrdome of thoſe that then were to dy. Firſt
of all there went many of them before
by ſix and ſix in a ranke : then came the
Martyrs ,

Martyrs, the handes of the men being
fast bound behind them, the womens
foote. The little *Iames* intreated very
hard that they would tye his hāds as they
did the rest, and scarce could they quiet
him with telling him that there was neuer a cord to tye them withall. They
went one by one betwixt the Stewardes
or Prefectes of the Confraternity, with
lighed candles in their hands in significa-
tion of the light of faith in their minds
and burning loue of God in their hartes,
and after them a whole army of Christians, singing aloud the Letanies of our
Blessed Lady. A vertuous man one of
those that went in the company, did
offer to take vp *Iames* the little boy and
to carry him in his armes, but he humbly
refusing his courtesy, sayd : *I pray you let
me go on foote, for our Blessed Sauiour Iesus
Christ I take it, neyther went on horsbacke
nor in a litter to be crucified, and after this
little labour I hope I shall haue certaine and
eternall rest*. These wordes moued many
that heard them vnto teares, and made
the

the good man take vp the holy Child by
force, aud so he caried him vntil he came
vnto the place of Martyrdome.

18. Being come thither, whilest the
Officers were busy in binding them to
the pillars of wood, at the which they
were to bee burned, many came to take
their leaues of them, and to get some par-
cells of their garmentes to keep as Reliques: In the meane while one of the
Martyrs whose name was *Leon Canyemō*
stood vp, and spake aloud in this manner: *We be come hither, good people, to dye
in the manner you see for the honor and glory
of Almighty God, and because we knowe there
is no other meanes, nor way vnto saluation
but only by the holy Fayth of Iesus Christ,
and for it we ought not to make any recko-
ninge of this present life. All you Christians
that are come hither with so great feruour do
knowe this well inough, onely therefore we
desire you for a farewell that you perseuer in
the confession of this fayth, without making
any account in respect thereof of all that
is in this world, no nor of your very liues.* The
rest

rest which he speake could not be well
heard.

20.   After they were all bound to
their pillars, the Christians lifted vp
aloft, for the Martyrs and all the rest to
looke and meditate vpon, a very deuout
picture of our Blessed Sauiour as he was
bound to the pillar. Then the souldiers
putting fire vnto the wood and straw,
the Holy Martyrs in the middest therof
withall deuotion called vpon the help
and fauour of our Blessed Sauiour oftentymes, to that end naming the most
holy name of Iesus, and al the Christians
vpon their knees did sing the *Creed*, the
Pater noster, *Aue Maria*, and other praiers
vntill the Martyrs had giuen their Holy
Soules into the handes of God.

21.   *Iames* the little Child when the
ropes were burned with which he was
bound vnto his pillar, went treadingvpõ
the Coales towardes his holy Mother,
without euer offering to go out of the
fire as he might haue done: As he went
he sayd three tymes aloud *Iesus Maria*,
Iesus

Iesus Maria, and his Mother said vnto him, *looke vp my Child, looke vp into heauen*; and so he did, and then fell downe and dyed. The Deuotion also of his holy sister the Virgin *Magdalen* was much noted of some, and very worthily, for when her handes were loosed, the cordes wherewith they had beene bound being burned, she tooke the hoate burning coales, & put them on her head (for it is the custome of the *Iaponians* when they like any thing which is giuen them, to put it on theyr heades) in token that she did esteeme them as a Garland of flowers, and as pretious pearles, wherewith being crowned and adorned, she desired, and meant to meet her heauenly spouse, whome she loued aboue all other thinges, and therewithall she gaue her soule into his holy handes. *Leon Canyemon* making the signe of the Crosse, gaue vp the Ghost, and all of them made happy endes, their soules being as it seemed more inflamed with the fire of the loue of God, then their bodies scorched with

with the heate of the materiall fire.

22. The Christians who from the begining, as I sayd before, were al vpon their knees in prayer, seeing that the holy Martyrs were now all dead, reuerenced their holy ashes, and without regard of the officers leaped into the fire, & tooke out thereof the Blessed bodies, although therby some of them receaued no small hurt and domage by the fire. A man of worth got the handes of the holy Virgin & Martyr *Magdalen,* and the Christians of *Conzira* got her body: the other seaué were caried in Coffins to *Nangasaqui,* and there de'iuered to the Father Prouincial of the Society of *Iesus,* and withall possible solemnity, although not publique they were placed in their Church, the Bishop of *Iwoa, Don Luis Cerquyera* being there present at that tyme, and a little after the body of the holy Virgin *Magdalen* was brought thither also, and laid with the rest. So great was the deuotion of the Christians, that they neyther left pillar, nor coles that they did not take

take away for Reliques of them .

23 . The Lord Bishop made an authenticall information of al this history , according to the custome of the Church, and out of it was drawne that which is heere related . A little after vpon the 29. of October another man named *Thomas* was put to death for the same cause . He had beene banished eight yeares before out of the Kingdome of *Fingo* for the fayth of Christ , & at the present he had care of the Christians of a certaine town, and he did it with such care , diligence , and fruit , that many at his perswasion did confesse their fayth before the Iudges , and for that cause *Arimadono* comaunded him to be put to death , the which he endured very willingly , and calling continually vpon the Blessed name of Iesus, made an happy end .

I

How

*How this last persecution of all did be-
gin : and of the causes thereof.*

CHAP. V.

MATTERS passing in the country of *Arima* in the manner before related , there was all this
while no change at all in the Citties of
Meaco, *Fuximi* , and *Ozaca*, nor in the
Kingdome of *Canga* & *Noto* of *Bungo* &
Fixen , nor in *Aqui* a Citty of *Firoxima* ,
nor in *Nangasaqui*, and diuers other
townes , nor in the Ilandes of *Xiqui*, and
Cozura: The Churches there stood open
vnto all , and Gods Word was freely
preached therein , although they were
not without some feare and care to see
what that tempest which threatned som
greater storme to come , would proue at
length . They celebrated in the yeare
1613. the Night of our Blessed Sauiour
his Natiuity in all the places afore mentioned , with great solemnity, concourse
and

and deuotion of the Chriſtians . And v-
pon the 27. of December begon in *Meaco* the firſt Thunder-clappe and ſigne of
the future tempeſtuotis ſtormes ; *Itacuradono* the Gouernour of the Citty comanding that the names of all the Chriſtians
ſhould be taken and written downe in a
Catalogue , and the ſame was done in
Fuximi and *Ozaca* : the which caüſed no
ſmall trouble among the Chriſtians ,
eſpecially they not knowing the caüſe
and reaſon why it was ſo done , vntill at
length there came two letters , the one
from *Saſioye* , the other from *Xozamburo*
both of them great fauorites of the *Xogun* . The firſt was directed to the Father
Rector of the Society of *Ieſus* in *Meaco* ,
the ſecond to another Chriſtian a very
friend of his , both of them dated from
the Court vpon the eleauenth Moone :
and the contentes were , that it had
beene ſignified vnto the *Xogun* , that the
Chriſtian Religion was ſuch , that thoſe
that did profeſſe it , did neyther obey nor
eſteeme of their Maiſters , Lordes , nor

Princes, and that they did adore men put
to death for Malefactors, tooke their
flesh and bones for Reliques (as they
termed them) and wore them at their
neckes. And for proofe therof they related all that had passed about those
Christians which had been burnt at *Arima* , signifying that it had so beene told
vnto him. And that moreouer very many Christians did of late publiquely a-
dore a man that for his iust desertes was
crucified in *Meacc*. For al which he being
much offended said, that, that Religion which teacheth such doctrine, is
doubtlesse of the Diuell, and therefore
could not be tolerated in *Iapone*. In the
end they said that they were very sory to
send them so bad newes, but yet could
not chuse but let them vnderstand thereof.

2.   This blow did grieue the Christians very much, and to the end they
might better vnderstand how the matter
went, and procure some remedy thereof, after they had consulted amongst
them-

themselues, they sent vnto the Court a
Brother of the Society, a man very ex-
pext and intelligent, with intention that
Father Rector should also go thither to
that end soone after him. *Safioye* had
notice thereof, and meeting with the
Brother reprehended him exceedingly,
telling him moreouer, that now there
was no remedy, for that the *Xogun* had
giuen expresse Command that not one
of all those that taught the religion of
Christ, whether they were strangers or
borne in the Country, should remayne
in all *Iapone*, and that therefore he should
returne immediatly vnto *Meaco* from
whence he came.

3. The truth of the matter was,
that when *Safioye* came vnto the Court
he found that many there talked very
much of the 28 Martyrs that had beene
there put to death in the Moneth of August last past, as also of the great constancy of those that in *Arima* chose rather
to be burned aliue, then for one only
houre deny their fayth: of the courage

I 3   likewise

likewise of those Christians that went thither to see that spectacle, offering to dye with them, and how they reuerenced their Reliques. Some said it was too great a cruelty, and that it had beene inough at the most to haue banished them and confiscated their goodes : whereupon *Safioye* and others partly through the hatred they bare vnto the fayth of Christ, and principally for the excusing of their owne cruelties, did defame the Christians vnto the *Xogun*, as disobedient, stubborne and rebellious people, that they did not feare death, but rather did desire to be put to death as Malefactors, and that they do esteeme and adore such like persons ; and a brother of *Safioye* did giue this reason thereof, because said he, Christ whome they hold for their Lord and Sauiour did dye vpon a Crosse as a Malefactor.

4. But this proceeded from the late death of a Christian that was crucified in this manner. Seauen persons were condemned to death in *Meaco*, for hauing bought

bought vncoyned siluer, as it seemeth,
against some law of the country to that
effect. Six of them were Gentills and the
seauenth was a Christian. The Gentills
were beheaded, the Christian was crucified. Many people according to the
custome of all places went to see the execution, and when the Christian gaue vp
the Ghost, the Christians that were
present kneeled downe vpon their knees
to comend his soule vnto God; and thereupon some of the Gentills, malicious
persones, tooke occasion to giue out
that they did adore him that was crucified. And to excuse their cruelty towards
those of the Prouince of *Arima*, they
exagerated the matter, saying that if one
only Prouince was so obstinate, that
there was no remedy to make them obey
neyther their Prince nor the *Xogun*, what
would it be if the greater part of *Iapone*
were Christians, as already they were
very many in *Meaco*? adding withall
that as long as the Fathers were permitted in *Iapone*, it was not possible there

I 4   should

should be any remedy therein .

5 .   Thefe and the like thinges they
did paint out , and exaggerate in fuch
manner to the *Xogun* and the Prince his
fonne , who before were nothing well
affected , but rather auerted from the
Chriftians by reafon of the falfe reportes
of the Gentills and Heretikes; that they
refolued to banifh all the Fathers out of
Iapone, and cruelly to perfecute the Chriftians thereof : faying , that the Fathers
as being ftrangers and religious perfons
were not much to be blamed for preaching of their religion , feeing it was
their office and profeffion fo to do ; but
that euery Prince and Lord were worthy
to be blamed that did permit the to liue
and preach in their Countries ; & much
more the Chriftians there , that gaue
eare vnto them , and did more efteeme of
the doctrine that was taught them by a
few ftrangers , then of that with their
anceftors had profeffed, & their Princes
did imbrace and cõmand to be belieued
& followed , and that therefore they did
                                    only

only banish the Fathers without doing
them any other hurt, or harme, but only
depriuing them of their Churches and
Houses: wheras those that were free De-
nizens should be secretly punished if they
did not obey. And so the Catalogue was
first to know how many Christias there
were in those places, & then by that to
procure that they should all of them
leaue their fayth: which was the selfe
same manner they had vsed before with
those of *Yendo*.

6. ¶ All possible diligence was vsed
by the Christians to see if they could by
any meanes make the *Xogun* capable of
the truth of matters falsly feigned against
them, and to giue him a true Information of the Catholique fayth. But the
Princes of *Iapone* are of that nature and
disposition that if once in any thing they
be resolued, they scarce euer afterwards
do change their mindes; neither is there
almost any that will, or dare make intercession vnto them for another, although
it be in a matter the most iust that may

I 5   be

be, especially if the enemies of that person be in fauour with the Prince, and
themselues be not to receaue some benefit by the busines. Whereupon it came
to passe vpon the 12. of February 1614.
that notwithstanding al the meanes that
could be wrought, there was an expresse
order made that al the Fathers in *Iapone*,
with al those that did belonge vnto them
should be sent to *Nangasaqui*, and there
deliuered vnto their Superiors, and vnto
the Gouernors of the Citty, & that their
Churches, & houses should be cast down.

7. Vpon the 14 of the same moneth
this order was notified vnto the Fathers
of the Society of *Meaço*, for that there
was no other Church but theirs in that
Citty, and they were required to giue vp
a Catalogue of the names of all the
Fathers, Brethren, and *Doxucos*, or Se-
ministes, as also of the seruantes they
had, to the end that none of them should
remaine behind. But because it was very
necessary that some should stay secretly
there for the helpe of the Christians of
that

that Citty , and of other townes and villages there about, of eight Fathers they
put only three in the Catalogue , and of
seauen Brethren other three , and of 20 .
Seminaristes only six .

8.   Those three Fathers and their
company were banished out of *Meaco*
vpon the 21. of February, and there was
an infinite concourse of Gentills to see
them (for the Christians were not permitted by the officers to go:) some mocked at them , others tooke compassion of
them, considering the innocency wherewith they had liued amongst them so
many yeares . When they were come into
Fuximi they found the Fathers of the
holy Order of *S* . *Francis* that did dwell
there already put in baotes ready to depart, and there they were all deliuered to
a seruant of the Gouernor of *Meaco*, that
was appointed to carry them to *Nangasaqui* . Downe the riuer they went and
came to *Ozaca* before the breake of day,
and there were ioyned vnto them others
of the Society , and of *S.Francis* his order
that

that did dwell in that Citty, as allo another Father with others of the Society that were brought from the Kingdomes of *Canga* and *Noto* : so that vpon the 25. of that month there departed from *Ozica* a reasonable fleet of banished persons for the faith of Christ.

9. Before their departure Father Rector did offer vnto the Gouernors of *Meaco* and *Ozaca* a memoriall in which he answered to the false calumniations which were raysed against the Christiã fayth and Religion, desiring them they would shew it vnto the *Xogun*, and informe him of their innocenty. Both of them did read it, and sayd that which was therin conteyned stood with very great reason, and that they thought that if the *Xogun* did se it he would desist from persecuting the Christians. By the same order that those already mentioned, were also banished the Fathers of the Society that dwelt in *Firoxima*, and in the Kingdomes of *Aqui*, *Bingo*, *Bungo*, and *Figen*, of the country of *Omura*, the Ilandes of

Xiqui

Xiqui, and *Conzura*, as also before had
beene in the yeares 1612.and 1613.thofe
of *Bugen Chicugo*, *Chicugen*,together with
the Fathers of *S . Augustins* order of *Vsu-
qui*, and the Fathers of *S . Dominicke* of
the Kingdome of *Fyen* . Finally in all *Iapone* there did not remaine fo much as
one Church which was not caft downe
and deftroyed, all the Religious men being brought to the port of *Nangafaqui*, except fome few that lay hidden
and went fecretly difguifed in diuers
partes .

10 .   The Society had at that time
in *Nangafaqui* foure feuerall Refidences,
the Colledge and Seminary all in one ,
the *Mifcricordia*, the Hofpitall, and the
howfe of All.faints, and other two they
had not far from thence: there were alfo
three Couentes there, one of *S. Augustine*
his order, another of *S . Dominicke*, and
the third of *S . Francis*.There were more.
ouer foure parifh Churches of fecular
Prieftes that were *Iaponians* borne, befides other leffer Chappells.The number
of

of the Churches that were destroyed in all partes of *Iapone*, may be gathered by that which the Society alone did loose in the yeare 1612. when the persecution did but begin in *Arima* (although it were not vniuersall) which were foure-score and seauen Residences, Churches, and Chappells. It would be to tedious a matter to write in particuler all the mo-lestations & vexations which the Chri-stians receaued vpon this occasion, to-geather with their valour, courage, pati-ence and constancy therin, the which is nothing diminished by the frailty which some exteriourly did shew, seeing that it is no nouelty that some in all places be not so constāt in religion as they should: euen in *Europe* it selfe where Chrstian Religion most florisheth, and is of most continuance we haue to many examples thereof, yea and which is more in the very primitiue Church of Christ, there neuer wanted some, that were vncon-stant, cowardly, to too fearefull, & faint harted.

Of

Of that which happened in Meaco *and* Ozaca .

CHAP. VI.

MEACO is the moſt populous & ancient Citty of *Iapone*, and the ordinary Court of the *Dayri* , who by right is the true Lord of all thoſe Kingdomes . It is the very well ſpring & fountaine of al the Idolatry of that coun- try , and hath in it many Temples and *Bonzoes* . *Fuximi* is another Citty di- ſtant ſix miles from *Meaco* , although it be now almoſt ioyned with the ſuburbes thereof . It was builded by *Taycoſama* the predeceſſor of the *Xogun* that now reig- neth , who hath there a goodly great for- treſſe , and it is his Garriſon towne for the partes of *Camy* . There he hath con- tinually 6000 . ſouldiers vnder the charge of 4. Captaines, and the Generall of them all is *Oquindono* who is his owne brother. *Ozaca* is 20. miles lower down the

the riuer towards the West , and is also a
very populous Citty, hath many goodly
Pallaces in it, & one of the best fortresses
if not the best of all *Iapone*. *Taycosama* did
build it, and his sonne *Fideyori* doth dwel
in it to this day . *Sacay* is six miles more
towards the South , and the Inhabitants
thereof be all Merchantes and Tradef-
men .

2 . In euery one of these Cittyes there
were good store of Christians , and all of
them , especially those of *Meaco* and *O-*
zaca, where were the greater number ,
hearing of this newes did endeauour to
moue themselues to feruour and deuotion. The two Gouernors *Itacuradono* and
Ichinocami did desire to put as few Christians into the Catalogue as might be ,
partly because they saw it was a manifest iniustice that was intended towards
them , and partly least they themselues
should be blamed and rebuked for that
there were so many . But all the Christians , euen the very Children , would
needes haue their names written in the
Catalogue

Catalogue; for that in *Meaco* alone there were at that tyme more then fower thouſand, whoſe names were taken. Some there were that were then but only diſpoſing of themſelues in Catechizing to be Chriſtians, and were not yet baptized, that did put in their names among the reſt, and more then threeſcore at that very tyme were baptized, notwithſtanding all the troubles likely to enſew, affirming that they ſhould hould theſelues for very happy to dy in ſo holy a religion : and among the reſt an ancient woman of threeſcore and ten yeares old, that had very often reſiſted vnto Gods calling and holy inſpirations giuen her to be a Chriſtian, a very little before the departure of the Fathers was baptized, to the great contentment of her ſelfe, and all her Chriſtian freindes.

3. There was a little Child in *Sacay* who ſaying to his parents that he would be a Martyr with them, and they telling him, that if he could not ſuffer a little ſparke of fire on his hand, how would he

K   ſuffer

suffer greater tormentes, he tooke a hoat
burning iron to try it in his hand if he
could endure it: his parentes detayned
him, but could not quiet him vntill they
promised him they would carry him
with them when they went to dy.

4. There was another young youth
nephew to a certaine *Bonzo* whose Téple
and Benefice he was to haue inherited,
and becaufe he made himfelfe a Chriftian, his owne Father hung him by the
feet and whipped him cruelly, but for
all that he would neuer leaue infifting
that they fhould put his name downe in
the Catalogue of Chriftians, becaufe he
was he faid a Chriftian, and fo would
liue and die. For which caufe his Father
did difinherite him, and violently thruft
him out of his houfe, and he went imediatly to the Fathers of the Society, making earneft fuite to go away with
them.

5. All this tyme there was an extraordinary concourfe of the Chriftians vnto the Churches, notwithftanding all
the

the floutes and mockes, and reprehen-
fions of the Gentiils : much frequenting
of the Sacraments and prayer, and the
prayer of forty houres was almoft continually kept in many places: and it was
the generall care of al by meanes of thefe
holy exercifes and diuers penances they
did, to prepare themfelues to dye . They
were much grieued to depart from their
fpirituall Fathers & maifters, not knowing whether they fhould euer fee them a-
gaine or no, and fo great and grieuous
was their lamentation for this refpect ,
that the very Gentills tooke great pitty
and compaffion both of them and the
Fathers alfo , faying publikely , that the
officers that hindered them , did them
great wrong and iniury not to let them
go in their company, feeing they did fo
much defire it .

6. Vpon the 16.of February *Sangamidono* one of the principall Captaines
and Tutor to the Prince of *Yendo* came
to *Meaco* with a hundred and fifty horfe-
men, and many more on foote vnder
pretence

pretence to pull downe the Churches,
and destroy the Christians, although as
we shal see heerafter the *Xogun* had another intention therein . The next day
following , he commanded to cast downe
the Church and House of the Society,
and to carry the wood thereof to the riuer side , making a Proclamation that all
that would not deny their faith should
be burned with that wood , and that e-
uery one should prepare his pillar of
wood whereunto to be tyed when they
should be burned . Many immediatly got
them pillers and set them ready at their
dores , others that had no money to buy
them withall, sould some of their house-
hould stuffe , because when the tyme
came they would not be without them.

7.   And they in this manner expecting the happy day of Martyrdome, the
foresayd wood was commanded to be
burned publikely , togeather with the
wood of two other Chappells , and of
the Churches of *Ozata*, *Fuximi*, & *Sacay*
to the great griefe and affliction of all
the

the Chriſtians , and thereby they came
to vnderſtand , that all that had beene
done was only to terrify and put them
into a feare . For *Sangamydono* and the
Gouernors of *Meaco* & *Ozaca* ſeing their
inuincible courage , determined firſt of
all to aſſault them by meanes of their
freindes , neighbors and kinred , and if
that did not preuaile , then to diſgrace
ſome of them publikely , and to blot out
of the Catalogue the names of others
eyther by force, or by deceipt, to comply
in that manner with the *Xagun* , thinking to giue him notice oly of thoſe that
were in their iudgments moſt rebellious
and obſtinate .

8. Preſently hereupon the neighbors, freinds, and kinſfolkes of the Chriſtians begonne to enter in troupes into
their houſes , ſome breaking downe and
tearing in peeces the pictures of our
Sauiour and his Saintes , ſome taking a-
way their beades and *Agnus Deis* , and all
other ſignes of Chriſtianity they found:
others partly with threates, partly with
K 3   intreaties

intreaties and importunities , infifting
that at the leaft they would confent that
their names might be blotted out of the
Catalogue . This Combat did endure
a good while and diuers were the euentes
thereof . Few were ouercome : a great
number eyther by force or by decept had
their names blotted out of the Catalogue : and the moft conftant were mi-
ferably vexed and affli&ed.

9 .   There was in *Meaco* a certaine
ftreet called the ftreet of the Chriftians ,
becaufe al that dwelt therein (except one
only family) were fo , with thefe they v-
fed extraordinary diligence to make
them leaue their fayth , and becaufe they
could not preuaile with them, they banifhed two families as heades of all the reft,
and then in the fight of their husbands
and fathers they put 27 . perfons , women and Children , into certaine fackes
of ftraw into the which they vfe to put
their rice , and tying them with cordes
round about from top to toe , they caft
them one vpon another , as though they
                                         had

had beene lackes of corne , and afterwardes , becaufe they fhould not be fmo-
thered,they laid them in the ftreets vpon
the ground ,leauing them fo for all men
to behold a whole day and a night , in
exceeding cold weather and fnow , with
men to keep them , who continually
did importune them that they would
yeald at leaft in fomething or other . But
for all this , and all they could do , they
could not ouercome them . Yea other
children there were that wept and cried
very ferioufly , becaufe they were not
put and tyed in fackes as their mothers
and their fifters were ; and to quiet them
there was no other way but to put them
in , where withall the Gentills did remaine aftonifhed .

10 .   The day following the Iudges
did returne, and affirming that the huf-
bandes of thofe women were not men ,
feeing they were not moued with the
difgrace and punifhment of their wiues
and children , they commanded they
women to be loofed , and the men to be

tyed in the sackes, and put to the same
torment that their wiues were put vnto
the day before, threatning them that if
they did not deny their faith they would
cause them to be carried in that manner
vpon a staffe through all the streetes of
the citty, to their publique shame igno-
miny and disgrace. But by the grace of
God they made small reckoning of their
threates. Then came there thither a great
troupe of Gentills, who first, giuing
them many reproachfull wordes and
speaches, did afterwardes intreat the
Iudges that they would deliuer thē into
their custody, & that they in their houses
would giue thē such counsaile, as should
be conuenient for them. And so it was a-
greed, because indeed they were loath to
fill the prisons full of Christians; whose
wordes in all this tyme were nothing
but protestations, that they would so
remayne (by the assistance of the holy
Ghost) vntill their dying day.

11. Neere vnto the Church of *Meaco*
there liued in a house all together very
recollectedly

recollectedly diuers Gentlewomen that
had made vowes of Chastity in the company of a noble Lady called *Iulia* , sister
vnto *Don Iohn Naytodono* , of whome
shortly we shall make mention . This
Lady remayning widow after the death
of her husband who was a principall
Lord of the Kingdome of *Tamba* , left
the world being yet a Gentile to be a *Bi-*
cuni , which is a kind of religious life a-
mong the Gentills , and so she remained
for the space of fourteene yeares , liuing
in great pouerty and penance , spending
her time in doing many heathenish rites
and ceremonies , for the which she was
greatly esteemed of many of the most
noble Ladies of all the Land , and of all
of that sect which she professed , although
the longer she liued in that fashion the
lisse quietnes she found in her Conscience . It pleased Almighty God to open
her eyes as another *Lydia* in the actes of
the Apostles by hearing the sermons of
the Catechisme which were preached by
a Brother of the Society who was a *Ia-*
K 5   *ponian*

ponian borne : and allthough her ancient custome and the speach of the world weighed very much, and were great impediments to hinder her conuersion, yet the grace and calling of Almighty God being more potent and powerful, within a short tyme she came to see the error of the *Iaponian* Sects wherein she had beene very conuersant, & to know the truth of our holy Christian and Catholike Religion, and was baptized by F. *Organtino* of the Society of Iesus in the yeare 1596 . after which diuers persecutions were raised against her by the *Bonzos* for leauing of their sect; and because she had burned certaine Idolls which they esteemed very much, they procured the *Xogù* to made enquiry after her , to punish her therefore; and vpon that occasion she was forced to liue secretly diuers yeares. She gaue herselfe wholy to deuotion and became thereby to be so good a Christiã and so spirituall , that she together with her company did exceeding much good among the Gentills , teaching the Christian

stian Religion to diuers Ladies & Gentlewomen whome they visited, to whom
no man could possibly haue any entrance
or accesse , and by her meanes many
soules were deliuered from the Diuells
power , and her howse was as it were a
place of refuge for the Christian women, such was her vertue, such her wisdome, such the good example she gaue
to all.

12.   The Iudges togeather with the
Gouernors. Nephews were fiue daies in
endeauouring to make these good
Gentlewomen leaue fayth, sometymes
by faire means somtymes by foule; and
finally for a conclusion they tould them
that hauing vnderstood that the Christians did desire to dye for their religion, they were resolued not to fullfill
their desires therein, but otherwise to
afflict them by all meanes possible, and
afterwardes cause then to be carried
naked through the streetes of *Meaco* to
their publike shame, and then to banish
them into diuers partes , so that they
                              should

should neuer see one another more, and to such places where they could not liue as Christians, & that all this they might easily remedy with dissembling a little exteriourly, and consenting that their names might be blotted out of the Catalogue. They answered they would not, and that if they did blot out their names by force, they would publikely proclayme that they were Christians.

13. The Iudges went away, and the good Gentlewomen afterwardes did expect euery moment when the officers would come: at length there came a whole troup of them, and the holy women went out to meete with them, each carrying a sacke in her hand, into which presently the officers did thrust them, and bynd them so hard that they could neyther moue hand nor foote, and then they tyed them to staues and so carried them vpon their shoulders through the streets accompanied with many armed men. The people came all out of their houses to see them, some mocking

at

at them and abusing them , others admi-
ring at their constancy . They put them
in a publike place without the Citty ,
where they vse to execute Iustice vpon
malefactors, and their they remayned all
that day and the next , exposed to the
could and snowy weather. Great aboundance of people went thither to see them,
and among the rest a certaine *Bonzo* ,
who comming ful of pride and presumption said vnto them , that they were ignorant women , that they should rely vpon
him who was a learned man , and that
he would take vpon him their saluation :
they laughing at his folly gaue him no o-
ther answere, that being sufficiēt to con-
found his proud presumption . Certaine
Gentills did procure to deliuer one of
them , and by force did carry her from
thence vnto her Fathers house , but she
went all the way crying out aloud , *I am
a Christian*, I am a Christ̃i, and when they
let her go she tooke vp the sacke and the
ropes wherewith she had beene tyed in
her handes ; and neuer ceased (running
                                    through

through more then ten ftreetes, till fhe came againe to the place where her companions were, and there fhe made her felfe to be bound againe as they were, to both her owne and their great ioy, confort & content. The next day the Iudges fent word to loofe and let them go, but they vnderftanding that it was a deuife thereby to giue out to the world that they had now yealded, they faid, *We are Chriftians, and will not go from hence, vnleffe you go proclaiming that we wil not leaue our holy fayth and Religion, and if you will not do fo, let vs remaine heere vntill we dy*. As they required fo was it done, for they tooke, and tyed them, and carried them backe againe through the fame ftreetes they brought them, proclayming that they ftill remayned Chriftians, and themfelues likewife did proclaime the fame faying all the way, *we are Chriftians, we are Chriftians*. They brought them to a houfe of a certaine Chriftian, and there they left them giuing them backe againe their beades, and *Agnus Deis*.

14. Others

14 . Others were in other ſtreetes likewiſe put into ſackes, and among the reſt one that was named *Benet* ſhewed particuler feruour in that action : for being put into a ſacke within his owne houſe, & ſo tyed that he could not moue, he cried out vnto them, that they ſhould put him in the ſtreet for all to ſee him ſo, and at length he obteyned his requeſt, but it was in ſuch ſort that his face was couered : he was much greeued thereat, for his deſire was to be mocked and re-proached for Chriſts cauſe : and becauſe they would not diſcouer him, hauing oftentimes intreated them, he himſelfe with his head and teeth by force made meanes to diſcouer his face, which when the officers perceaued they carried him in againe, & put him into a ſtrong priſon of wood, ſo ſtraite that they could ſcarce put any meate in to hin . There he re-mained vntill he was baniſhed . This tor-ment of tying in the ſackes was ſo great, that moſt of them, or all did fall ſicke therof.

15 . In

15 . In *Ozaca* was the same affliction and persecution, as in *Meaco* , and the constancy of the Christians there no lesse then in the other place. Those that went abroad about any busines left at home in writing how they were Christians, & that if there were any torments to be inflicted for being so , they would returne presently to suffer them . Others that were abroad when the newes was told them of the persecution , left presently their businesse for the same end. Some young youthes were most cruelly whipped by their parentes for being Christians , and shut vp without any meate at all for a long tyme. Then arose a report that vpon a certaine day , at such an houre , the Christians should be put to death , in such a market place . Whereupon diuers of them did begin to giue all that they had vnto the poore : and vpon the day appointed before the hour came, there were more then three hundred come and expected in the place , and many more there would haue beene, had they

they not beene then by force deteyned
by their freindes and kinsfolkes. Fifty
and eight were put in sacks in the manner afore rehearsed & so carried through
the streetes, vnto a great bridge vpon
the riuer, where they were left fast boūd
and diuers persons appointed to keepe
them; the rest were beaten away with
cudgells, yet as they went, they did not
cease to make publike profession of their
fayth, saying, *We are Christians.*

18. Amongst those that were put
in sackes there were some Gentlemen of
good worth who had thrust themselues
into the thronge among the common
people, because they would not be fauoured nor exempted: and a Nephew of
the chiefe Lord of the Kingdome of *Aua,*
whose name was *Iohn Xiroyemon* and his
wife *Magdalen* no lesse noble then he,
she being then very great with child &
hauing been banished a yeare and a halfe
before thither for their fayth, were both
of them there also in the market place a-
mong the other Christians.

L   17. That

17. That very night certaine Gentills came and asked that those that were put in sackes might be giuen vnto them, and that they would be their suerties, but the Christians refused their courtesy, because it might be thereupon suspected that they had yealded to something that they ought not to haue done: at length they let go the ordinary people and put 24. of the better sort into diuers prisons.

18. In a towne neere vnto *Ozaca* the Gentills did take a Christian, and because he would not deny his fayth, they first pulled of all his clothes, bound him to a piller, and for two dayes together they burned him by little and little with dry reedes and straw (the which they vse insteed of torches) so that he could not dy of it, because they would not do him the fauour to make him dye for Christ as he desired: and being not able to ouercome him with all they could do to him, they banished him together with other of his kinred that were Christians.

19. The

19. The fury of this persecution did endure for ten daies space, and at the end thereof, there came from the Court letters in which the *Xogun* did declare *Sangamidono* for a Traytor, and comanded that he should imediatly be banished into the Kingdome of *Omi*, and that he spared his life in regard he had beene his Captayne so long tyme. And this was the reward of all his malice against the Christians. And it was afterwards proued, that, that very day in which he pulled downe the Churches, that very day was his Castle of *Ondauara* seized on, & all his landes and liuinges which were very great, confiscated. The Gentills themselues some of them did note how soone he was punished for his cruelty.

20. For conclusion of this Chapter I thinke it will not be amisse, to relate a witty and pleasant prognostication which as they say was made in *Meaco* at this tyme, by a Gentill, one of their Southsayers. For he casting a figure vpon this manner of proceeding, neuer

seene

seene before of putting the Christians into sackes, said these words: *The sackes be of Rice, & Rice is a seed that multiplyeth very much: a signe, that though they presse the Christian neuer so much, they will greatly multiply*. The Gentills made a Iest at it: but some Christians thought that perhaps there was a greater mystery therin then was imagined.

Of some in Meaco, Ozaca, *and* Fuximi *that were banished for Christian religion, and others imprisoned.*

CHAP. VII.

THE Christians of *Meaco* and *Ozaca* remayned prisoners, a moneth. But how great their valour courage and deuotion was therein may well be gathered out of a letter which one of them wrote vnto a Father of the Society in this forme: *Vpon the eight day of this Moone they brought me vnto this prison, with my wife and three Children: I beseech you remember me in your holy Sacrifices;*

crifices , and obteyne for me by your prayers
of Almighty God, perseuerance . We are not
vnmindful of those good consideratiōs which
you taught vs : and although we be miserable
sinners, yet we do our endeauour euery day to
communicate spiritually , remembring our
selues of the holy Sacrifice of the Masse . We
do also giue thankes dayly vnto Almighty
God for his exceeding benefitts . We feare no
persecution, nor esteeme our liues in any thing
at all ; and this strength which we find and
feele within our selues, we acknowledge it for
Gods fauour , and the fruit of your care in
teaching vs, and we giue you thanckes for all.
I vnderstand that all our companions stand
very stedfast in their fayth , of the which we
are exceeding glad : we are not forgetfull
of them neyther day nor night . And so once
more desiring you would comend vs to Almighty God , and giue vs your blessing , I
end .

2 .   After this came the *Xoguns* sentence in which he comanded that all the
prisoners with their wiues and Children
should be banished to *Taugaru* , which is

at

at the end of al *Iapone*, a very cold Countrey, ouer againſt *Tartaria*, and ſcarce
inhabited , and that thoſe Gentlewomen which liued all together in one
houſe in *Meaco*, ſhould be ſent with o-
ther ſeauen or eight to *Nangaſaqui* to be
baniſhed from thence out of *Iapone*, and
that thoſe whoſe names were blotted out
of the Catalogue ſhould be compelled to
follow ſome of the Sectes of *Iapone*.
There were ioyned together from *Meaco*
and *Ozaca* vpon the 13. of Aprill threeſcore and thirteene, who were deliuered
vnto two Captaines to be carried into
baniſhment: but they ſeeing them to be
ſo many, and that ſome of them were
knowne to be worthy and noble Captaines, were afraid to take the charge
of them ſo long away: and therefore they
intreated *Itacuradono*, that eyther he
would comand irons and fetters to be
put vpon them, or els ſome marke with
fire to be made in their for-heades wher-
by they might be knowne, and taken a-
gaine in caſe they fled away from them.

Itacuradono

Itacuradono laughing at them, said: It
seemes you do not know them, nor the
willingnes & contentment with which
they go into banishment. I should be very glad I could deteyn the for the compassion I haue of them. Goe with security, for those that goe in the manner that
they do, will not run away I warrant
you. Take my word, for I knowe them
very well.

3. It so happened, that the Officers bringing threescore and thirteene
horses for them to ride vpon vnto a
place where they were to take shipping,
one horse was ouerplus by reason that
a little boy that was one of the forsaid
number being hidden by his kinsfolkes,
was wanting: and the Officers reflecting
vpon it, and saying that one of them was
wanting, a young youth that was come
thither to take his leaue of some of those
that were to go into banishment, hearing
them, stept out and said; *Here I am, take
no care there is none wanting*, and saying
so, he leaped vpon the spare horse, and

with

with great content went along with the
reft into banifhment.

4 .   They went all in a row one after
another , moft of them very richly appa-
relled, and exceedingly content . Whereat many of the Gentills wondred not a
little , feeing that in their conceipt they
had reafon rather to fhew griefe then
any contentment at all in that occafion . Diuers Chriftians, accompanied
them to *Otzu* , with teares and a kind of
holy enuy , emulating their happines in
fuffering that which they did for Chrift.
And they all that way went aminating
thofe that were to returne and remaine
there behind, not to fhew any weakenes,
frailty or cowardize in Gods caufe , nor
to feare neyther loffe of goodes nor life ,
feeing that all in comparifon of euer-
lafting life is but of fmall , or of no account.

5 .   The Fathers of the Society that
liued at that tyme fecretly and difguifed
in *Meaco*, the better thereby to help the
Chriftians, did very much defire to haue
                                    accom-

accōpanied thefe their Ghoftly children,
but it being both neceffary for the greater good of others not to difcouer themfelues , and daungerous to do it , they
therfore fent a good Chriftian , a *Iaponi-*
an borne, vnto them in their names , a
man of much vertue and great confidence to help and animate them in their
iorney , who willingly with all his hart
did vndertake that care , being indeed
himfelf defirous to dye with them . They
ftayed in the port vntill the middeft of
May , expecting wind to fayle the Nor-
thern Seas . Thither in that tyme many
Chriftians went to vifit them , and by a
letter which one of them wrote vnto a
Father of the Society of *Ozaca* may be
gathered the manner of their going, and
how they did behaue themlelues : thus
he wrote .

6 . *Vpon the* 22 . *of the third Moone*
(which was vpon the 30 . of Aprill) *I*
went to vifit the banifhed perfons which then
were in Tzurunga: *& I remayned fo edified*
by them , that I do affure you I felt in my-
felfe

*selfe extraordinary shame and confusion, ac-
companied together with deuotion. All of
them both men and women had caused the
hayre of their heads to be shauen of: euery day
three seuerall tymes they made their prayer
altogeather, and at euery tyme they spent an
houre therein: they had so distributed matters
among themselues, that euery one did some
office or other to help and serue the rest.
When they came to* Tzurunga, *they were
all put in a great warehouse, the dores fast
locked vpon them, and there they passed all
that night vpon the cold bare ground: and
exceeding glad they were, that therein they
did in some manner imitate the martyrs, of
whose afflictions and torments they did discourse amongst themselues. The night following they had giuen them two matts to
lye and sleep vpon: their meate whilest they
remayned there, was a little rice with pottage
made of certaine hearbes, that were (God
knowes) of an vnpleasant tast. The Captaines
that conducted them said once vnto them :
Because you were many and most of you skill-
full in matters of armes, we made some difficulty*

culty at the first to vndertake your conduction,
but now seeing your manner of proceeding,
we see we had no reason at all to feare . And
verily with this resolution you haue shewed in
choosing rather to be banished then leaue your
fayth , you haue giuen an euident testimony
that it is the truth , and the right way vnto
saluation: and if you had not done so , you
had put a great blot vpon your religion , and
giuen testimony that all which it teacheth
were false and vntrue : and doubtlesse if the
prohibition of the Prince were not so strict as
it is, we would heare the sermons of so good
and holy a doctrine . This and much more I
might write vnto you, of that which the Captaines sayd, moued with their good example .
Hitherto the letter .

7 . They departed afterwards from
that port , and ariued safey at the place
whereunto they were banished , & there
as was after signified , they were well
receaued and also holpen by the Prince
thereof . The Gentlewomen whereof I
spake before , together with others were
sent in banishment to *Nangasaqui,* where
they

they were releeued by the charity of the
Confraternities, especially by that of the
Misericordia. Some also were banished at
this tyme from *Fuximi*. There was also
one *Peter* a were graue man and an an-
ciēt souldier much respected by *Oquindono* the *Xoguns* Brother, who had endea-
uored much to make him leaue his fayth,
and not obteyning it, he sent him word
that it was the *Xoguns* pleasure, that ther
should not remayne one Christian in all
Iapone; that the Fathers were now banished and the Churches destroied; & that
he could do no lesse but banish him if he
did not leaue to be a Christian: to which
he answered: *I did not make my selfe a
Christian because there be Fathers or Christians in Iapone, but because I knewe there
was no other way to saue my soule. I am very
sorry that they are banished, and that the
Churches be destroyed: but yet I knowe that
he that brought thē from the furthest partes
of the world hither, can more easily bring thē
againe from* Macan *&* Iuson *which is nee-
rer*. The Xogun *can do no more but put
them*

them out of his Country for his owne tyme:
and if he will banish me also, I shall find God
I am sure wheresoeuer I go, for he is I knowe
in all places wheresoeuer. And for conclusion he desired him not to speake any
more vnto him about that busines, but
eyther banish him, or command him to
be put to death: and so both he and other
soldiers of worth that gaue like answers
were banished with their families, their
goodes, and liuings being all confiscated.

8. Amongst the Cittizens of *Fuximi*
was most persecuted one *Marke Mango-*
bioye a man of good account and much
esteemed of the Gouernors, and other
of the *Xoguns* fauorites; they vsed extraordinary diligence to make him releng,
but not being possible they banished him
withall his family vnto *Nangasaqui* He
told them he did accept of it, but yet
that was no banishment seeing they sent
him thither where the Fathers were.
Some frends of his that were Gentils did
secretly entreate the Gouernors that they
would

they would diſſemble with him for a
while, & that they would be his ſuerties
that he ſhould conforme himſelfe. The
Gouernors were very wel cōtent withal,
but he hauing notice thereof went vnto
them ſaying, *That he was a Chriſtian, and
that he would not leaue to be ſo for all the
world, and that therefore they might reſolue
eyther to kill him, or baniſhe him as they
pleaſed.*

9.   They were much grieued therat
but there being no other remedy they
ſent him to *Nangoſaqui*, doing him the
fauour not to confiſcate his goodes.
Scarſe was he arriued there, it being
200. leagues from whence he went, but
there came letters vnto him from *Meaco*
that *Marina* his wife & her litle daughter
ſhould preſently returne to *Fuximi*, but
not ſignifiyng wherefore, nor for what
cauſe it was. They were all much troubled therewith, and very loth to part one
from the other, but yet for all that they
returned according to the commaund
both of them with great reſolution firſt
                                        cutting

cutting off their haire. The Gouernors
did intend eyther by threats or flatteries
to make *Marina* yeald at leaft a little, &
then by her meanes winne her hufband
to their will, but fhe anfwered very conftantly, *that although they fhould kill her,*
or make her a flaue to be a drudge al the daies
of her life in a kitchen, fhe would not change
her minde. The Gouernors with this fo
vnexpected anfwere remained as it were
aftonifhed, for they thought infallibly
that fhe would eafily yeald, feeing her
felfe alone, without her husband, and
forfaken of her friendes, and thereupon
they let her go: and fhe and her daughter
returned both very ioyful to *Nangafaqui*
hauing now made three iorneyes each
of them 200. leagues a peece.

10.   In *Meaco* the officers had blotted out the names of diuers Chriftians
in the Catalogue, of fome by force, of
others by fraudulent, and deceiptfull
meanes, the parties themfelues fome of
them openly repugning thereunto; o-
thers being content to winke thereat,
but

but hauing afterwards great fcruple of
Confcience, they went vnto two publique *Officers*, called *Choday*, protefting
vnto them that they were, and are ftill
Chriftians, and that it was contrary to
their willes that their names were put
out of the Catalogue, leauing with them
in writing their names and the ftreetes
wherein they dwelt. One of the *Choday*
diffembled the matter with them, and
bad them, if they were Chriftians, they
fhould be wary for feare of the *Xogun*.
The other was more rigorous, & caufed
thereupon *Peter Chobieye*, *Gyroyemon*, *Ri-
yemon*, and others to the number of 13.
to be put in prifon. *Peter* and his mother
were banifhed to *Tzugara* for their fayth;
the reft after many affaults were carried
togeather with their wiues and children
before the Gouernor, where a principal
perfon ftepping forth and asking them
why they hauing once left their fayth,
did not performe their wordes and keep
their promife, but returned againe to
profeffe that which once they had forfaken:

ſaken : *This is the cauſe* (ſayd they) *why
we come hither to let you and all the world
knowe , that we neuer left to be Chriſtians,
and that for our religion we are ready to ſuffer torments , yea and death it ſelfe* . Thereupon they laid hold on them al, & bound
them with ſuch cruelty that their hands,
their neekes , and armes did ſwell exceedingly : and *Itacuradono* , fearing that all
the Chriſtians would do the ſame that
they had done , did reuyle them bitterly
and told them , that if they did not obey
he would command that the men ſhould
be carried about the ſtreetes to publique
ſhame , and the women to the ſtewes :
and they all anſwering that they would
neuer obey in that matter, preſently they
tooke the women and carried them to
the foreſaid place , and the men through
the principall ſtreetes with a great and
ſtrange tumultuous noyſe , and vpon a
little bord, in a paper, their ſentence written thus : *For being Chriſtians hauing once
left their fayth* ; the which was falſe . But
ſo they left them tyed all that day in a

certaine little market place for all to laugh and mocke at them, and within few houres after *Iohn Yosiyemon* & *Iames Mangaxichi* were taken and carried in the same manner.

11.   Three of the Seminary of the Fathers of the Society went to them imediatly to animate & encourage them, & another went to the street called the Christians street, to warne all to make the prayer of Forty Houres to God for their perseuerance. That night they were carried backe againe to prison, and there they lay with irons at their neckes. The next day they were carried to the bridge of their street, there to be tyed to the postes of it, and because the officers should vse no mercy towardes them, the Iudge said vnto them : *Looke that you do as I comand yon, for the Gouernour is exceeding angry that you tyed them so gently this lastnight, that two or three of them hath not the skinne rubbed of from their neckes with the ropts. Tye them hard inough, and if they dye of it, it makes no matter, I will beare*

you

you harmelesse . With this the officers vsed
themmost cruelly , and tyed them vp so
highthat they did scarce touch the gro-
und with the tipps of their toes , byn-
ding moreouer their neckes so strait that
they were almost strangled.Three dayes
they vsed them in this fashion , the Gentills and the *Bonzos* comming thither
continually to perswade them to accommodate themselues vnto the tyme: but
they little regarding their perswasions
said vnto them : *Looke vpon vs , and vn-*
derstand that to suffer that which we do
willingly, and with the ioy you see is a suffi-
cient signe,that in our religiō there is meanes
of saluation . After they had done all
this with them , they carried them backe
againe to prison , in which from Iuly of
the yeare 1614. vntil March 1615. when
this Relation was written they did remayne suffering with great constancy in
their fayth, & ioy in their afflictions .

12 .   The valour of their wiues and
daughters in that infamous place whereto they were sent, was in my mind wor-

thy eternall memory , for to the end
that no man that looked vpon them
should lust after or desire them , many
of them did disfigure their owne faces,
making them all on a gore blood , with
little woundes they made in them . For
which cause their handes were after
tyed ; but the Christians vsed a good de-
uise to get them out of that place to be
kept in the house of an honest Christian,
where they did hitherto remayne firme
in fayth and constant in their good purposes . With these and the like examples
those Christians that had shewed some
weaknes before , were moued to do
pennance for their fraylty and incon-
stancy , and afterwardes to be more constant & couragious, as in particuler it shal
appeare of one *Paul Fioxayemo*, of whose
Martirdome we shall make mention in
the 14. Chapter of the second part of this
relation .

Of

Of the banishmēt of Don Iusto Tacayama
and of other Gentlemen of Focoru. *&*
of the Christians of Firoxima .

CHAP. VIII.

SOME fiue or six . dayes iourney
Northward from *Meaco* , doe stand
the Kingdomes of *Canga, Noto* , and
Yetehu, the prince whereof *Figenaono* was
very much affected to the Christian religion , and vsed the Fathers with great
respect and curtesy

2 . He had in his Kingdome diuers
noble Christian Captaines and in particuler *Don Iusto Tacayama Minaminobo* ,
whose memory is famous in the histories
of the Society of Iesus of the *East Indies*
and *Iapone* , and *Nayto Don Iohn Toruan*
who was Lord of almost al the Kingdome of *Tamba :* and *Nayto Don Thomas*
Vaemodono his sonne , and *Oquinada Tho-*
mas Quicuan a principall Gentleman of
Bigen . *Don Iusto* had alwaies with him
M 3 some

some Father of the Society, and a Brother, and others of the Seminary that was in the Citty of *Canazoua*.

3. When the newes of the persecution came first into those partes, *Don Iusto* did determine to keepe the Father secretly, to the end he might help the Christians there in case they came to dye for their fayth, as all did hope and desire they should. But presently there came a comand from the *Xogun*, that the Father and those that were with him should be carried by officers vnto *Nangasaqui*, and so it was of necessity put in execution : but before his departure so great was the concourse of the Christians to confesse themselues, to receaue the Blessed Sacrament, and to take their leaues of him, that the Church was scarce euer empty eyther day or night. Three dayes after his departure together with the rest of his company, *Figendono* did by order from the *Xogun* comand (though much against his will) that *Don Iusto*, *Don Iohn* and *Don Thomas* with their Wiues, Children

dren

dren and Grandchildren ſhould be caried to *Meaco*, and deliuered to *Itacuradono*, and that all their ſeruantes ſhould be baniſhed if they did not leaue to be Chriſtians. Great was the aſſault that was giuen them there to'accommodate themſelues vnto the tyme, leaſt otherwiſe they ſhould vndoe themſelues, and vtterly ruinate their Families, which were of ſo great name, fame, and nobility. But they as men experienced in ſuch like Combats, hauing loſt before at other tymes, and ventured for their fayth, more then they could do now, were nothing moued therwith: ſaying that to honeſt men, and ſuch as know what it is to be Chriſtians, no man ought to mention any ſuch matter, no not in way of ieſt or merriment.

4. One only day was giuen them to prepare themſelues towards their iourney, and ſo leauing their landes, liuings, wealth, weapons, howſes and eſtates, without any more then their only apparell on their backes, and ſome thinges

neceſſary

neceſſary for the way, they tooke their
iorney to *Canozua* vpon the 15. day of
February. So *Don Iuſto* like another *A-
braham* left his Country, togeather with
his wife *Iuſta* and fiue *Grandchildren*,
(the eldeſt whereof was 16. yeares old
and the yongeſt 8.) and his daughter
who was married vnto the ſonne and
heire of the Gouernour of thoſe three
kingdomes, a man worth forty thouſand
ducats by the yeare. This Lady for diuers reaſons, and principally becauſe ſhe
deſired to dy in this occaſion with her
Father, went with him ; her huſband
being very willing therewith. He was
alſo a Chriſtian, and deſired much to
haue accompanied his Father-in-law,
but for iuſt occaſions he would not permit him. And ſo hauing made a generall
confeſſion of all his life with a Father
of the Society before his departure, he
remained there expecting what would
be the euent of theſe troubles, with in-
tentiõ if God gaue him life to ſend after
for his wife, and both of them to dy togeather

geather for the faith of Christ .

5. When they went out of the Citty
the Gentills did feare there would haue
beene made some vprore, by reason *Don*
Iusto had so many seruantes , freindes ,
and wellwillers there, and that all the
world saw euidétly the manifest wrong
and iniustice that was done to him , and
the rest , and therefore they did arme
themselues to preuent whatsoeuer might
happen . But he sent them word , they
needed not to feare , saying : *That now he*
was not to fight with weapons as at other
tymes they had seene him do , but with pati-
ence and humility , as the Law of God doth
teach. Many people did accompany them
a little on their way , some weeping to
see such men that were a little before so
rich and so esteemed in the Kingdome,to
go now out of it in banishment,in pouerty and with officers to guard , them, not
hauing done the least offence or committed any fault at all. Others admyring
to see such courage and constancy in
them,sayd:*Doubtlesse the Christian religion*
must

*must needes be very good, seeing that men of
so good Iudgment & vnderstanding as these
be, so wise, noble and valiant do for it so litile
esteeme, and so lightly regard their liues, &
make so smal account of their goods, honors &
estates.*

6.   At the end of the first daies iorney
it was told them, that some were comming towards them with order to put
them all to death, the which when they
heard, with great ioy and gladnes they al
setled themselues to their prayers, without making the least signe of sadnes, or
shew of resistance in the world : but rather when afterwards they vnderstood
it was a false all-arme, they were very
sorry, and grieued that it proued not so
as it was reported.

7.   After ten daies iourney they arriued at *Sacamoto*, three leagues from
Meaco, hauing endured much misery in
the way passing ouer many high hills &
craggy mountaines full of snow, which
they could not go ouer but on foot : and
Don Iusto being so old as he was, & sicke
withall,

withall, was yet still the first, animating
so much the rest that euen the children
and yong damsells which neuer before
knew what hardnes meant, went with as
great contentement ouer those mountaines, dabling in the wet, and trampling
in the snow, as if they had beene wal-
king in stately Pallaces, and pleasant
galleries.

8. *Itacuradono* vnderstood of their
comming, and fearing that if they should
come into the Citty, the Christians
thereof would bee to much ecouraged,
he wrote vnto the two Captaines that
garded them that they should stay in *Sacamoto* vntill they had further order frō
the *Xogun*. It seemed vnto *Don Iusto* that
their sentēce would be one of these three
thinges : eyther that they should be put
to death there, or els carried to *Yendo &
Suruga*, and there made an end of with
torments and disgrace, or finally banished vnto diuers Kingdomes, that so
being separated one from the other, they
would assault them euery one by themselues

selues to make them leaue their fayth, telling them that the rest had conformed themselues and condescended to their will. And this last he feared most of all by reason of the children and women that were among them, least they therby might be circumuented, & for that cause he did preuent them with instructions, bidding them they should not giue any credit to such like false reportes : and wishing thē also that though they should heare that their owne parentes, and all other Christians had denyed their fayth, they should remanyne yet constant and perseuerant, seeing that, that was the only and secure way to saluation.

9.   At the end of thirty dayes, there came a sentence from the *Xogun*, that the men should be banished to *Nangasaqui*, and that the women if they would might remaine in *Meaco*, but that they should not carry any seruantes at all with them. The women would not part from the men, but went with them; and in the iourney, which did endure 20. dayes, for

for want of ſeruantes, and vpon other
occaſions, they paſſed much miſery and
incomodity, yet at length they ariued
all at *Nangaſaqui*, and were there very
well receaued.

10. There were beſides theſe diuers
other principall Gentlemen baniſhed frō
Canozaua, and ſent to *Tzugarum*, and in
particuler *Thomas Quiucan* with his three
ſonnes who were men growne and alſo
of good eſtates. This *Thomas* was one of
the principall Captaines of the prince of
Bizen, and of two other Kingdomes.
He had beene of the ſect of *Tocquexus*,
and ſo obſtinate therein, that although
his ſonns and freinds were moſt of them
Chriſtians, yet was it not poſſible to
make him leaue his Sect, vntill it pleaſed
Almighty God to open his eyes in the
yeare 1600. by meanes of a Father of the
Society. But afterwards he became ſo
feruorous and deuout a Chriſtian, that
he was an example to them all. He had a
certaine faire Grange wherto he often
retired to recollect himſelfe, to giue himſelfe

selfe to prayer, to read good bookes, and
do diuers kind of pennances. *Figendono*
did esteeme of him so much that he made
him one of the foure Iudges of all his
Estate, and for this cause greater were
the assaultes that were giuen vnto him,
and his Sonnes: but they defended themselues so manfully, that they with three
other Gentlemen rather chose to loose
their goodes, rentes, and reuenues, and
to be banished out of their naturall soyle,
then to yeald in any the least thing a-
gainst their fayth.

11.   In the same Citty there was a
chiefe Noble man, who hauing diuers
seruantes that were Christians, did vse
many perswasions to one of them that
he would leaue it. But he answered: *If
it please your Lordship, I am so conuinced
with the force of the truth of our religion,
that it is impossible for me to leaue it: neyther in being of it do I you any iniury at all,
but rather thereby am bound and obliged to
serue you with more fidelity.* His Lord was
so offended with this answere that he
stroke

stroke him with his dagger, and wounded him, and meant to haue killed him
with another blow, and had done so,
had not some there held his hand, and o-
thers taken away the valerous Cham-
pion of Christ, who there vpon his
knees stayed expecting and desiring
it.

12. In the Citty of *Firoxima* matters were carried after a calmer sort, by
reason that *Fucuxima Tayudono* Lord
thereof, and of the Kingdomes of *Aqui*
and *Bingo* was a freind vnto the Christians, and fauored the Fathers of the Society very much, not only giuing them
ample licence to make Christians in his
Country, but also (being a Gentill himselfe) gaue them a house and place wherein to dwell, and part also of their maintenance: and so by that meanes there
were many worthy Christians in his
Countryes. But letting passe the fruit
which those of the Society did in those
and other neighbour Countries at that
tyme, I will now only speake of that
which

which passed there in the tyme of this
persecution .

12.   In the beginning of February of
the yeare 1614 . *Tayudono* being at the
Court of *Yendo,* he wrote a very curteo-
ous letter vnto the Father that was superiour at *Firoxima,* saying that he was very
sory for their banishment , but now it
could not be remedied being so ordeined
by the *Xogun,* & that he would be mind-
full of them. He also wrote vnto his Gouernors, that they should send the Fathers
withall courtesy to *Nangasaqui* ; and that
as touching the Christians they should
not medle with any but of the common
sort , and with those only for comple-
ment and fashion sake. The *Gentills* there
when they heard first the newes of the
Fathers departure were very sory for it ,
and came vnto the to signify how much
it grieued them , for indeed they all did
loue and esteeme them very much : but
there being no remedy , one of the Fathers
with others of their house remayned
there secretly , and the rest departed to
Nangasaqui.

Nangasaqui . The Gouernors tooke from the Christians their beades, pictures and *Agnus Dei* , and put some of them into sackes as those of *Meaco* had beene , and afterwardes making relation to *Tayudono* of what they had done, and carring vnto him some of the Christians beades , he said that they had done to much, & commanded the beades, *Agnus Dei,* and other thinges to be kept with reuerence as holy thinges .

13 .   This *Tayudono* is one of the Princes of most Fame in all *Iapone* , a notable warriour and a man of great resolution and courage in his businesses : and because he had emulatours in the Court, he wrote vnto foure of his Captaines that to giue contentment to the *Xogun* , he desired them they would leaue their religion , and that therein they should do him great seruice . They answered , *that they desired much to dye in his seruice , and that they were very sorry that in that matter which he demanded they could not giue him contentment. For that setting a side that*

N   *which*

which was the principall (to witt their fayth
to God, their Religion and Saluation) euen
in morall honesty and worldly honour, being so
knowne for Christians as they were, they
could not now pull backe their feet, but that it
would be a base and dishonorable thinge, and
a signe of a false hart & cowardly mind, neyther would any men of worth, if they should
goe from their fayth, euer afterward put any
trust or confidence in them. That which they
could and would do, was to be carefull whilest
they remayned with him in the Court not to
make any exteriour shew of their being Christians, by which any hurt or domage might
come vnto him: and that if this were not
sufficient, they, their wiues and children were
prepared rather to dy then to do any thing a-
gainst the profession of their Fayth. It was
thought that *Tayudono* would haue been
much offended with this answere : but
he did dissemble the matter, rather esteeming them the more for it.

14. This Prince had a Christian
page, who was much molested by other
pages to make some signe that he was no
Christian,

Christian, and to this end they feigned
that his Lord did send vnto him for his
beades and *Agnus Dei*, but he would not
deliuer them by any meanes, wherewith
they being much vexed to bring him
into difcredit with his Lord, they tould
him how they had now drawne him to
deny his faith. Within a few dayes after
his Lord asked him if he were a Chriſtian, becaufe it had beene tould him that
now he was none: & the page anſwered:
My Lord, I am a Chriſtian as you know, and
haue beene allwayes from a chyld, and for all
the world I will not leaue to be ſo. I do defire to
ſerue your Lordſhip in all you ſhall command
me, but to deny Chriſt that may not be : and
if for this caufe your Lordſhip will cut of my
head, heere I offer it very willingly; and
with that he did vncouer his necke. All
that were preſent thought aſſuredly his
Lord would haue cut of his head, for
that in ſuch occaſions many tymes he is
not Mayſter of himſelfe : but yet at that
time he did bridle his paſſion, & prayſed
his pages refolutiõ, who by that meanes

remayned

remayned with victory ouer the Diuell,
and his other enemies, and was in more
fauour with his Lord, and more esteemed of then before.

Of the Christians of Bungo: *and of foure*
therin that gaue their liues for the
fayth of Christ,

CHAP. IX.

CHRISTIAN religion did florish very much in the Kingdome of *Bungo* in the tyme of
King *Francis*, both in the number of
many noble Christians, and also in the
many Churches which the Society of Iesus had there. But after his godly death
his sonne *Yoximune* being banished by
Taycosama, all that noble company was
dispersed into dyuers places, although
they perseuering in their fayth were occasion that others where they were did
the same. The Society in this Kingdome
had three Residences, in *Facata*, *Notzu*
and

and *Xinga* , whither the Christians of
other places did resort . These also tasted
of the same cup that those of other places
did , the Fathers being banished , and
their Churches ouerthrowne. But before
they went many came to confesse themselues from many leagnes off, and to
aske aduise concerning their soules busines : diuers there were also (although
there wanted not some that were not so
constant) that notwithstanding all
threats and intreaties , remayned very
strong ; and many thinges there happened of no small edification , and worthy
to be remembred .

2 . The Officers ordayned that seauen persons , two men with their wiues,
and three Children should be carried to
their publique shame through the streets
round about the Castle , the space of
a league almost. And one of them called
Benet went all the way disciplining himselfe , and at the going vp of a steepy hill
he said to another Christian : *O how wea-*
risome would this affliction be if we did suffer

it

it for our owne willes, or for worldly respectes.
But our B. Sauiour for whose sake we vnder-
goe it, doth make, that we feele it not. To him
be giuen infinite thankes for his mercy shewed
vs heerin.

3. There was made neere the way
side a little yard or court, and after their
passing through the streetes they were
put therein, and then sackes and cordes
and all other thinges being ready prepared, they were put into them, and
bound therein as those of *Meaco* before
had beene, and so cast one vpon another,
and *Benet* put vnder them all. And with
a thicke cane (in which he had vsed to
keep holy water) they did bynd and
presse his hands so hard before his brest,
that for a whole day and a night, in
which they held him in that fashion, it
was a most cruell torment vnto him, &
he was so much weakned therewith
that the officers for feare he should haue
dyed, carried him (he being not able to
go himselfe) to the house of a certaine
Christian: where when they had vn-
loosed

looked him, they began to perfwade him
to leaue his fayth, and becaufe he would
not, they carried him backe againe to
the place from whence they had brought
him, bound and tyed him as he was before, and there he remayned in that
manner till the next day: and then feeing
that he was ready to giue vp the Ghoft,
they carried him againe to the fame
houfe as before, where he calling vpon
the holy name of *Iefus* gaue vp his happy
foule into our B. Sauiours hands the 7. of
April 1614. And becaufe the Chriftians
fhould not reuerence his holy body, they
drew and dragged it to the riuer fide,
there burned it, and caft the afhes into
the water. But a Chriftian making as
though he fifhed, tooke out fome of his
bones that were not confumed with the
fire & caried them to *Nangafaqui*, where
the Fathers of the Society that had conuerted and baptized him did bury them
with all reuerence and decency conuenient.

4.   This *Benet* was borne in the
N 4   Kingdome

Kingdome of *Izuno*, in his youth he
had been a *Bonzo*, and liuing in *Don Iusto*
his Country he was conuerted to the
fayth of Christ, together with his May-
ster and diuers of his Schoolefellowes:
his wife children and companions remayning so constant that the officers
seeing that in all that tyme and withall
their tormentes they could not ouercome them, they let them loose and cast
them out of the country, and so they
went to *Nangasaqui*.

5. At the same tyme three other
Christians called *Clement*, *Michael*, and
Linus (the two last being sonnes to the
former) all substantiall men, were much
vrged that they should leaue their fayth;
and not preuayling with them, the officers let them alone: but soone after there
came order from the Court from *Inaba-
dono*, Lord of that towne, that in any
case they should compell the Christians
to fulfill the *Xoguns* comand: whereupon
Clement gaue a note vnder his hand vnto
the Officers, that he and his sonnes
                                    wholy

wholy renounced Christianity . His
sonnes when they vnderstood thereof
were much afflicted , and went imediatly
vnto the Gouernour , saying , *That they*
were Christians , and that the note made by
their Father was altogether without their
consentes : and that if he would giue them
leaue to liue as Christians , they would not
make any exterior demonstration of it : but if
not , that then they were there ready to suffer
any torments , yea and death also for their
fayth . The Gouernour answered that he
had sworne neyther to fauour , nor to
dissemble in any sort with the Christians , yet for all that, he would take counsaile and aduise in this busines .

6. Not longe after the Officers came
armed to their howse and tooke them al
three , and *Maxentia Michaels* wife also ,
and his two children , and they carried
them al to the Castle, and there put them in
prison euery one by theselues alone spa-
rated from the rest,thinking thereby the
more easily to conquer the & make yeald
but all in vaine : for they could not ouer-

N 5   come

come any of them no not euen the little
Children. *Linus, Maxentia,* & her sonne
Peter were put in sackes, and there being
peeces of sharp pricking strawes left or
put in the sackes as it seemeth to torment
them the more, one present would haue
shaked them out of that sacke in which
Maxentia was to be bound; but she
would not permit him saying, *That, that
torment was but very small, and that she
wished she had many bodies and liues to giue
for her God & Sauiours sake.*

7. *Peter* first animating his mother
and his vncle *Linus,* then spake vnto
the Gentills in this manner: *I warne you
all that no body do giue false subscriptions in
our names that we leaue our fayth; for if
you do, I will go presently to* Meaco *to giue
notice thereof vnto the Gouernor, and he will
hold you for falsifiers when I shall tell him
that we alwaies haue been & are Christians.*
Linus being in his sacke and saying his
prayers something aloude, some of the
Gentills did put a gag in his mouth of
clouen canes, and tyed it like a brydle
about

about his chinne , and although afterwardes moued with compaffion they
tooke it away , yet he earneftly entreating them to let him haue it ftill , they
eafily agreed thereto , and let him fo remaine for two whole dayes together.
One that was there prefent did much defire to make him relent , and to that end
he carried him to his houfe , and there
both he and his wife did intreat him euē
with teares that he would leaue his religion , for two or three dayes only , pro-
mifing if he would do fo not only to procure him life and liberty , but that they
would alfo giue him good ftore of mōey
befides : but he little regarding their
offers , tould them they labored in vaine
and fo they returned him againe to the
prifon with his brother *Michael* , where
they both of them remayned preparing
themfelues to dy for Chrift : and from
thence they wrote fome letters to their
friends abroad full of humility and re-
fignation into our Sauiours handes . By
this one of *Linus* his writing , we may
gather

gather the manner of the rest .

8 .   *This I write from the prison where
at this present I do remaine through the grace
of the holy Ghost : and although a wretched
and miserable sinner , yet hauing my hope &
confidence placed in the mercy of Almighty
God , I do most earnestly intreat you would
pray for me vnto him , our Blessed Lady , all the
Saintes , and happy soules of heauen , that I
may perseuere vnto the end . Although vnworthy yet was I put into a sacke and so remayned one day and a night because I would
not deny my fayth , and after that they put
me in prison with my Brother Micael . I am
determined and resolued by the grace of God
and the help of your good prayers to perseuere
euen vnto death in the seruice of my Sauiour.
Once more I beseech you to pray for me vnto
God to giue me perseuerance , for I am a great
sinner , and haue no other confidence but only
in his diuine goodnes . This sixt of the sixt
moone .*

9 .   After 7 . dayes vpon the 13 . of
Iuly these two holy brethren were adiudged to be burnt aliue , which was very
                                 ioyfull

ioyfull newes to them , in ſo much that
when they were taken out of priſon ,
Michael ſaid to *Linus* : Is it poſſible that
only we two be ſo happy as to dy for
Chriſt ? deſiring much that his Father
wife and Children might be companiōs
with them in their crowne . And in part
Almighty God did ſatisfy his deſire : for
that Officers taking his wife *Maxentia*
out of the ſacke in which ſhe yet remained , they carried her to the place were
he and his brother were to be burned ,
to ſee if with the ſight of their torments
ſhe would any thing relent : ſhe ſeeing
her husband was exceeding glad hoping
ſhe ſhould accōpany him in that happy
death . In the way diuers Chriſtians wēt
to meet them , and ſaluted them with
great reuerence , deſiring they would
pray for them vnto God . As they paſſed
by the place where *Benets* body was burned , *Michaell* made a low reuerence
therto as to a holy place . They went all
the way (which was about a league)
bare foote, and one of their ſeruants offering

ring them shoes, they would not accept of them, saying : they rather desired that for that little space their feet might be cut and mangled with stones, that so they might suffer something for the loue of God. And *Maxentia* although she was a heauy woman not accustomed to go on foot, and hauing beene foure dayes togeather bound vp in a sacke, yet she wet barefoot all that way with so great contentment, that the very Gentills did admire her.

10. Comming to the place of execution, they found three pillers of wood set vp, whereat they were to be burned the which they imbraced, & then praied for the space of halfe an houre : then the two brethren giuing their beades and reliquiaries vnto a Christian that was present, because they would not haue them burned, put of their vpper garméts and each of them betooke himselfe vnto his piller, wher vnto being tyed, and fire put vnto the straw and boughes and other dry wood about them, *Linus* saying

Iesus

Iesus Maria , and *Michael* reciting of
his Creed, both their eyes being lifted vp
and fixed fast on heauen, they gaue their
happy soules vnto Almighty God .

11.   Whilest this was in doing there
were some that earnestly importuned
Maxentia , that at least exteriourly shee
would make some shew or signe to haue
left the faith of Christ . But she would
not, rather much desiring to dy for côfes-
sing it, making offer three seueral times
to go into the fire, but they stil deteyned
her with a rope which they had in their
hands fast tyed vnto her necke : and being not yet altogether out of hope to
make her yeald , they carried her to a
howse thereby , where they perswaded
her most vehemently . But she still answering that she was resolued , and that
to vse perswasions to her in that matter
was but labour lost , they carried her
backe againe to the place of Execution ,
where a soldier putting his sword twice
vnto her throat fiersly threatned to kill
her if she did not yeald, whereat she said:
This

This is a goodly threat inded, feeing there is nothing that I do fo much defire as to giue my life for the loue of God. If you fhould tell me that you would deliuer me, and fet me fre, that were the greateft thing that you could threaten me, for I hauing feene my husband dy with fuch valour and courage for his Lord and God, how can I enioy life but with great forrow, griefe and affliction.

12. Which being faid fhe tooke her haire that hung down vpō her fhoulders and backe, and caft it before to the end it fhould not hinder the blow of the axe, and then with an inuincible courage bidding the executioner do his office, calling often vpon the B. Names *Iefus* and *Maria*, fhe held out her head whileft he did cut it of. They burned her bodie prefently, which being done they tooke the afhes together with thofe of her hufband and his Brother *Linus*, and put them into fackes as alfo the earth of the place of their Martyrdome, & caft them into the deepeft place of all the riuer, becaufe the Chriftians fhould haue no-

                                                    thing

thing at all of them, no not of the earth
.where they suffered, to reuerence as reliques, although there wanted not some
that afterwards found meanes to get
some of them which they carried to *Nangasaqui*, and deliuered vnto the Fathers
of the Society.

13. A sister of these glorious Martyrs of Christ that was present at their
death gaue notice vnto their Father *Clement* of all that had passed therein, desiring both him and her Nephew *Peter* to
perseuere constant in their sayth imita-
ting so worthy an example, telling them
withall, that if they did shew feare and
cowardize, that besides the falling thereby into disgrace with God, they could
neuer after shew their faces euen before
men. *Peter* was alwaies very constant,
and although his Grand-father *Clement*
had shewed fraylty as we signified before, now he was very sory for it, and
asked pardon both of God and men:
telling withall the Iudges, that he was a
Christian, and desired to giue his life

O

for

for Chrift , as his fonnes and daughter-
in-law had done : but they being fatiffi-
ed with what he had already done, gaue
him leaue to go at liberty, and liue as he
lifted himfelfe.

14.   I will conclude this Chapter
with two other thinges by which al may
perceaue the conftancy and feruour of
the Chriftians of this Kingdome of *Bun-*
go . There was a worthy Souldier much
importuned by his Lord, by meanes of o-
ther perfons , that he would accomodate
himfelfe vnto the tyme for the prefent ,
and becaufe he loued him very well and
was loath to loofe fo faythfull a feruant ;
feing others could not preuayle, he went
himfelfe in perfon to perfwade him. The
fouldier vnderftood thereof, and leauing
behind him his fword & dagger (which
otherwife they alwaies vfe to weare) he
went out of his houfe to meet him , and
faid : *My Lord, I am refolued not to leaue to*
be a Chriftian, becaufe I hope in this religion
to be faued . If your Lordfhip come to per-
fwade me the contrary , it will be but loft
labour ,

labour, and if you please you may cut off my head for it : and therewithall he held out his necke for him to cut it off. And he remayning in that manner, a little sonne of his of no more then nyne yeares ould, came out of the house and did the same that he saw his Father do, and after him his Mother and Grand-mother, with the selfe same resolution : wherewith the Noble man was so astonished that although he were a Gentill and noted for his cruelty, yet did he fall a weeping, & being ouercome with so great constancy, returned backe vnto his house, though after some few daies for feare of the *Xogun* he commanded the valorous Souldier to depart out of his Country: to the which he willingly obeyed (sory he had not obteyned the crowne of Martyrdome) going himselfe and all his family to *Nangasaqui.*

15. Another good Christian called *Titus*, a substantiall man, was in like manner persecuted by his Lord, who seeing his great constancy commanded

him

him to send him his sonne, a child of
nyne yeares old called *Matthew*. He sent
him presently: and within two dayes after feigning as though he had killed the
child with tormentes, because he would
not leaue to be a Christian, he sent vnto
him for his daughter *Martina*, who was
of 14 yeares: and imediatly he sent her.
Within a while there came another message vnto him from his Lord, that
Martina was also put to a most cruell
death, & that if he were yet so insensible
that with al this he would not be moued
to obey, he should send his other sonne
called *Simon* who was 16. yeares old,
and after that he sent for his wife called
Marina: and the valorous Christian
sent them all most willingly, saying that
he had rather loose wife, children, life
and all then the grace of God, or leaue
his religion: and his wife and children al
of them went with great content to
offer themselues in sacrifice. The Lord
put euery one of them by themselues a
part, and then set vpon them, both with
intreaties

intreaties and with threates , but being
not able to preuayle any thing at all with
them , firft they powred very could water all ouer *Marinas*, body: to her daughter *Martina* they gaue no meate at all in
three daies together , and *Simon* the elder
fonne they beat moft cruelly, and wrong
his handes behynd him ; all of them notwithftanding this perfeuering very conftant ftill. The Lord feeing himfelfe fo
ouercome , fent word to *Marina* , that
feeing her Children knew not what religion nor faluation meant, fhe fhould
make them leaue the Chriftian fayth ,
and with that he would hould himfelfe
content , and pardon both her and her
husband . She anfwered , that fhe had
offered to God both her owne and her
childrens liues, and fo fhe could not giue
them any fuch counfayle . They had
confifcated *Titus* his goodes before all
this happened , and for the finall refolu-
tion , his Lord fent him word by a Brother of his owne , with armed men , that
if he did not defift from his obftinate

pertinacy

pertinacy, it should cost him his life, and
one of his sonnes also at least : the which
was no ill newes to them, but rather
being much ioyed at the Message, they
all offered themselues most willingly to
loose their liues for Christ : but the Lord
seeing their valour, courage, and constancy changed his determination, pardoned them, and gaue them liberty to
liue as Christians.

*Of other three that were put to death for
the fayth of Christ in* Facata, *and*
Aquizuqui.

CHAP. X·

THE Fathers of the Society had
two Churches and houses in the
Kingdome of *Chicuyen*, besides
others which they visited now and then,
and one in *Facata*, which *Simeon Condera*
Lord of that Kingdome, and one of the
most valerous Captaines of *Taycosama*,
did buyld for his buriall place; and another

ther in *Aiuzuqui* built by his brother *Michael Sayemon Iouo*, both of them great fauourers and patrons of Christianity in *Iapone*.

2 . After the death of *Simeon Condera , Chicuyendono* his sonne succeeded in the possession of that Kingdome, and fauoured the Fathers & Christians much, who were many , and some of them of noble parentage. And although he were much molested and sollicited by the fauorites of the *Xogun*, and especially by *Safioye* that he should not permit Churches nor Fathers in his country , yet did he still winke at them during his vncle *Sayemondono* his life , who was alwaies a valerous defendour of the Fathers and Christians . But after his death when the *Xogun* and his sonne put the Christians out of their houses and seruice in the yeare 1612 . he being much more importuned then before, because he would seeme to comply with them , and withall conserue the Churches from being ruinated , he sent word vnto the Fathers by

O 4   foure

foure Gentlemen of his house, that he had
beene a long tyme sollicited from the
Court not to permit them in his Kingdome, and that he did alwaies excuse
himselfe in that his Father was a Christian, and had buylded that Church: and
because he bore them good will, by
reason he saw they came from the furthest partes of the world, for no other
respect or interest but only to preach
their religion, he had alwaies hitherto re-
sisted: but now that the *Xogun* had forbidden al Gentlemen and souldiers to be
Christiās, he could do no lesse then what
was requested: yet was he content that
Tradesmen and common people should
be so still, and that he therefore desired
them to send him a note of all the Gentlemens names that were Christians.

3. The Fathers gaue him thankes
for the fauour he shewed them, but as
concerning the note of the Gentlemens
names, they desired he would pardon
them, being so that they could not do it
because it was a sinne, and that they
comming

comming thither only with intention to
make Christians, if they should giue any
such note as he required of the, it would
be to pull downe with one hand what
they set vp with the other, and not to be
true and faythfull to those that put confidence in them. He sent another tyme
to vrge them, that they would giue it,
but they answering with good and cur-
teous speaches, resolued in no case to
giue it, although it should cost them all
their liues. Whereupon *Chicuyendono* de-
sisting from his enterprise, medled only
with some that were publikely knowne
Christians.

4. The yeare following 1613. he
went to the Court to visit the *Xogun*, according to their custome euery new
yeare, and there vnderstanding that the
Xogun was disgusted with him for fauou-
ring the Fathers, he wrote vnto Father
Prouinciall of the Society, that the Fathers should depart to *Nangasaqui*, and
that the Churches must be pulled downe
to giue satisfaction to the *Xogun* :but yet

that

that he would be content, that they
should visit the Christians of his country secretly : and so they did , and no o-
therwise . For although these Lordes
or Princes of *Iapone* be great and potent
Personages , and well affected to religion,yet the *Xogun* being opposite and contrary , they cannot , nor dare not resist
him , and so the best way was secretly to
do what good they could.Within a short
tyme after arose the persecution at *Facata* . It was there proclaimed that all the
Christians should come together to a
certaine place before a Temple ; whither
being come they vrged them very much,
and to terrify the Multitude with the example of a few , and shew themselues
punctuall and exact in performing the
Xozuns command , they determined to
vse some rigour with *Thomas Xozayemon*
and *Ioachim Xinden* , who were more
forward then the rest.

5 .   This *Thomas* was very feruorous
in animating the Christians with his
exhortations & example of pennance &
mortification

mortification to perseuerance in their
faith, & *Ioachim* for his vertue and good
life was much knowne and beloued of
all the principal persons of the Country.
He was a Father vnto the poore, and
being a Phisitian he cured them of almes.
No diligence was left vndone to moue
and make them accomodate themselues
vnto the tyme, but they answering that
in no case they could do it, were presently sent to prison, and there bound
with cordes very strait vnto two postes,
but seeing that therewith they were not
ouercome, *Chicuyendono* comanded that
they should be both of them hanged vpo
a certaine tree neere vnto *Facata*, and
so left there vntyll they did deny their
fayth.

6.   Vpon the 13. of March they did
hange *Ioachim* vpon the tree, which was
a very high Pyne, his feet vpward and
his head hanging towards the ground.
And in the same tree they did also hange
Thomas in the same manner, but something below *Ioachim*; and being in that
terrible

terrible torment they did animate one
the other with great ioy and alacrity.
Remember Brother Thomas (fayd *Ioachim*)
that which our bleſſed Lord & Saniour Ieſus
Chriſt did ſuffer for vs vpon the Croſſe , and
let vs giue him thankes for this fauour that
he ſheweth vs , in ſuffering ſomething to his
imitation òn a tree . And although wee vn-
worthy : yet in ſome reſpect wee do reſemble
S . Peter , who was crucified with his head
downeward . I was euen thinking ſo (fayd
Thomas) & the conſideration thereof doth
eaſe my paine which is nothing to that which
I do deſire to ſuffer for Chriſt .

7 . The day following there was
great concourſe of peopleto ſee them : &
ſome of the Gentills ſaying to *Ioachim ,*
that they wondered he would be ſo obſtinate as to ſuffer ſo great a torment for
a thing ſo vncertaine as ſaluation is ,after
a while he āſwered. *I held my peace a while*
as being buſied with God ,not much regarding
men : but not to ſeeme diſcourteous , and be-
cauſe they may not thinke that we do repent
our ſelues; I pray you tell me one thing: Thoſe
that

that haue receaued so many benefits, honours
and fauours of Chicuyendono, *as many of*
you that be present haue done, if they should be
brought to such extremity, that eyther they
must loose their liues, or els bee disloyall vnto
him; would they not choose death and whatso-
euer affliction els, rather then to be traytors
vnto their Lord? How then can wee being
Gods creatures, and hauing receaued so many
benefitts of him as he hath bestowed vpon vs,
deny him now for all the tormentes that be, or
can be inflicted vpon vs? With this answere
the auditors were al conuinced, and both
Christians and Pagans did commend it
much.

8. Three dayes well nigh did those
two holy men remayne in that manner,
hanging by the heeles, not hauing so
much as one bit of meat or drop of water
giuen them all that tyme. At the end
thereof the Officers still seeing them remaine so constant as they were, did let
them downe, and caused them to be fast
bound imediatly to a ladder, which had
a peece of wood put through it in forme
of

of a Croſſe . A Chriſtian asked them
how they did : *Ioachim* anſwered : *I ſuffered much when I was a ſouldier , but ſuch paynes as at this tyme I neuer felt before , for it ſeemed to me that I was ſawed through all my body, but I conforted my ſelfe conſidering that al my tormentes were nothing compared to thoſe which Chriſt ſuffered for me : & I did apply my paines to his in ſatiſfaction of my ſinnes .* Chicurendono ſeeing their conſtancy , and that with ſo prolonged and cruell a torment they could not be made to change their mindes , gaue order that they ſhould be beheaded : which ſentence being giuen they were imediately taken & carried to execution , to a place that was ſomething diſtant thence . *Ioachim* could not mooue himſelfe , and ſo he was carried thither vpon ſouldiers backes : and *Thomas* went on foot , both of them repleniſhed with ioy and gladnes . When they were come vnto the place , hauing prayed a little ſpace , the executioner cut of their heades , they in the meane time often repeating the holy
name

name of *Iesus* . Their bodies and heades
were conueyed to *Nangasaqui* & giuen to
Father Prouincial of the Society of *Iesus.*
Their holy death was a great encorage-
ment to the Christians, as their liues had
also beene an example alwaies vnto thē.
A *Bonzo* preaching in that Citty soone
after their death said in his Sermō to those
of his sect : Those men questiōlesse were
of great valour, & there can be no doubt
but that they are saued, seeing they suffered so much, and with so great quiet and
contentment , for their faith.

9 . When *Michael Saymoendono* was
Lord of *Aquizuqui* , through his great
zeale and feruour he was the occasion
that more then fiue thousand of his seruantes, souldiers, and tenantes were baptized in the space of two yeares , by
meanes of the Fathers of the Society.
After his death the Estate was wholy
changed , only the husbandmen and cōmon people remayning therein , who
were committed to the charge of an old
Bonzo a great enemy of the Christians .

He

He called them all vnto him, and commanded them to write their names in a
paper whether they would be Christiás
or no, and finding that the most of them
did subscribe that they were Christians,
and would so continue, he was much
troubled thereat, and publiquely gaue
out that they meant to rise in rebellion.
Whereupon there came thither from the
Castle of *Fucuoca* fiue Captaines with
300. souldiers, who although they saw
euidently that the report was false, yet
did they enter into their howses, tooke
away their beades, pictures, and other
such like thinges, which bare any shew
of things belonging any way to Christian profession; and not content therewith, some they punished with tortures,
others they banished, and therin though
some shewed weaknes, feare and frailty,
yet others, and the greatest part, stood
stedfast with notable côstancy; of which
the Gentills would take no notice, but
without all reason and examination of
particulers did publish that they had all
                                    denied

denied their fayth, and so they exercised
their fury only vpon *Matthias Xichirobi-*
oye, who was one of the formest in sub-
scribing that he was a Christian, and as
it seemeth foreseeing that which would
ensue, did therefore assoone as he retor-
ned home begin to prepare himself to dy
for the same .

10. Vpon the 14. of March the Gouernor sent some vnto him to perswade
him not to be so obstinate, nor to animate others to be disobedient to their
Superiours : and they entred into his
house very violently, and by force tooke
away his beades from him, the which
grieued him very much for the present,
he reputing it as great a disgrace, as if
they had taken his weapons from him :
but after a little consideration he sayd
vnto them : *The Fayth of a Christian doth*
not consist in his beades nor pictures, but in
the mind, & in the constãt profession thereof
which by the grace and help of God, I meane
to do before the Gouernor and Captaines, &
in part I haue done, as may bee seene by my

P   *subscription*

fubfcription which already I haue giuen. They feeing that they were not able to preuayle with him, went vnto the Gouernors Leiftenant, who prefently fent for him, and he being fet downe to dinner when the meffenger came for him, rofe vp imediately without eating any thing with great ioy, faying. Let vs go, for with the helpe of God I fhail go now where I fhall not need to eat any more.

11. The Leiftenant afked him if he had giuen his name that he was a Chriftian, and that he would not obey the *Xogun?* To which he anfwered refolutely *yes, and that he was in that mind ftill: and that they needed not to proceede further with him in more queftions and demandes, for that hee would not change from that for all the goodes of the world.* There they made him expect a while till they had examined fome others, and then they carried him to *Aquizuqui*, where the Gouernor and Captaines were: and in the way paffing by an Idoll called *Fachima* which

which is the Idoll of Warre, they threw
him downe vpon the groũd & beat him
cruelly, perhapps becauſe hee would not
worſhip it , putting a rope about his
necke, and pulling it ſo hard that he was
almoſt ſtrangled therewith, and could
ſcarcely ſpeake , yet as well as he could
he deſired them they would ſlacke it a
little, that with better quiet and atten-
tion he might cõmend himſelfe to God
in that little time he thought he had to
liue : they anſwered him that ſeeing he
had willfully put himſelfe therin, he muſt
now haue patience : *You ſay very well ſaid
he, for ſince I ſuffer this for the loue of God, it
is great reaſon I ſhould endure it patiently*
Afterwardes they offered him to looſe
the rope a little , but he would not , ſaying: *Let me alone, for I deſire to ſuffer ſomething for Chriſt in this little remaynder of
my life* .

12. Being brought before the Iudges
they asked him why he was ſo ſtiffe and
obſtinate in his opinion. He anſwered
becauſe there is meanes of Saluation in the
fayth

fayth of Christ, and none at all in any of the Sectes of Iapone: and because I do belieue (said he) *this to be the truth, I will suffer for it willingly this and whatsoeuer els:* Yf it be so (said they) why did you deliuer your beades, and subscribe your name that you left to be a Christian? *My beades said he, were taken away from me by force, and although therin doth not consist the being of a Christian, yet was I grieued so much therewith that it cost me good store of teares. I gaue my name vnto the Gouernour, that I am and alwaies will be a Christian, and if there be any other contrary to this, it is not myne but falsly forged. For that I haue neyther said nor written any thing contrary to it, nor euer will do by the grace of God.* Hereupon they thrust him out of the roome with great disgrace, and reuyled him exceedingly, saying among other thinges, that a man so peruerse and obstinate as he, could not be a good subiect to his Prince, and so they adiudged him to death: and imediatly he was carried to the place of execution, whither he went

praying

praying all the way , and being come
thither , he said aloud that all might
heare : *I dye most willingly with great con-*
tent and ioy for the fayth of Christ . Then
he made a short prayer , which being ended they cut off his head . It was proued
in the Authenticall processe which was
made of his death , that he pronounced
the holy Name of *Iesus* three seuerall
tymes after his head was cut off , and the
third tyme it was heard more distinctly
then the rest , the which caused great admiration in the standers by . His holy
head and body were carried afterward
to *Nangasaqui* , and there layd in the
Church of the Society of Iesus of All-
Saintes , where likewise be the bodies of
many other holy Martyrs.

P 3   *Of*

*Of the great Constancy of the Christians of
Arima : and how they prepared themselues to Martyrdome.*

CHAP. XI.

ARIMADONO perceauing
that with the torments, banish-
mentes and martyrdomes before
rehearsed the Christiãs were rather more
and more encouraged then otherwise,
and that the fyre wherewith some of
them had been burned did seeme to in-
flame the rest in feruour and deuotion,
fearing least for that cause he should
loose his Estate, and being deluded by
some that desired to succeed him in it,
he sent vnto the *Xogun* to intreat he
might be changed to another Kingdome, where he might haue no medling
with the Christians, because the more he
did torment them, the more constant
did they shew themselues, so that now
he knew not what to do with them. Before

fore an anſwere to his Letter came, he
heard the newes of what had paſſed a-
gainſt the Chriſtians in *Meaco* and
thereaboutes, and thereupon he cauſed
thoſe Churches which as yet remayned
ſtanding to be ouerthrowne.

2. Some Gentills did perſwade him
that the beſt meanes to make them yeald
was to cauſe their wiues and daughters
to be caried naked through the ſtreetes
to their publike ſhame. And ſo it was
determined, wherewith the Chriſtians
were exceedingly troubled, and afflicted. Some of them were of opinion that
the beſt courſe in that occaſion was to
ſhut vp all the women into houſes, and
that the men ſhould keep them there and
defend their honors with their liues, rather then expoſe them to ſo vile and dan-
gerous a puniſhment : but after taking
more mature aduice they ſent the principall perſons of the Confraternities vnto the Prince to deſire him they might be
puniſhed with the ordinary tormentes of
baniſhment, beheading, crucifying, bur-
P 4 ning,

ning, frying, and the like, and that they
hoped they should take all with patience
being suffered for the loue of God , & for
the obteyning of their soules Saluation :
but that to vse so vnusuall and indecent
manner of punishment, as that which
was determined , would not be well
thought of at the Court .

3 . Vpon this the execution was differred , and insteed thereof it was commanded that all those that would perseuere Christians should leaue the rentes
they had . Whereupon imediately Fifty
noble Gentlemen did leaue all that they
had with great courage and alacrity , remayning poore without house, lands, or
rents , or any reuenewes in the world .
Wherewith *Arimadono* for that tyme
was satisfied , expecting the *Xoguns* answere and *Safioyes* returne , who was the
Chiefe author of all this wickednes;
and in the meane tyme the Christians
prepared themselues more and more for
Martyrdome, those of the Confraternities renewing the oath which they had
made

made to be firme and constant in their fayth: doubling also their prayers and penances, and making the prayer of forty houres in diuers places. They also sent for a Father of the Society to come vnto *Arima*, who there in a very few dayes did heare the Confessions of more then 800. persons secretly: and which is worthy of noting, the very Children (the eldest amongst them not being fifteene yeares of age) had there made amongst themselues a Confraternity in the honor of *S. Ioseph*, wherein they made their determination, which in this manner they set downe in writing: *Although the persecutors do pull out our teeth and plucke of our nayles, giue vs the torment of the water, and burne vs aliue, we will neuer leaue the fayth of Christ which we professe.*

4. After that *Safioye* was come to *Arima*, he sent for the 12. Stewardes or Prefectes of the Confraternities. They all went very ioyfully, thinking doubtlesse that they were sent for to be put to death for their religion; many also besides

P 5   sides

sides went with them , to see if they could be partakers of their crownes , the rest remayned at home preparing themselues for the same. Being come , *Safioye* made this speach vnto them : Through your obstinacy in not obeying to your Lord & Prince, he is now in danger to loose his estate , whereas if you would leaue to be Christians as the *Xogun* commandeth , both he and you might remayne in peace and quietnes in your Country . Consider well of it , and know for most certaine , that if you do not conforme your selues , he will loose his estate and you shalbe persecuted exceedingly . To this speach of *Safioye* one of the Christians there present answered in the name of all the rest : *My Lord , we need not consider nor consult concerning this Matter , seeing that long ago we haue beene resolued therein . As concerning the conseruation of Arimadono his estate , it dependeth not vpon our being , or not being Christians ; for that being so , we shall be both more faythfull and more obedient vnto him then otherwise . And*

as

as we alwayes haue beene to his Father *Don Iohn*, so will we be to him, ready to serue him both with our goodes and liues. But as concerning those thinges which touch the saluation & good of our owne soules, there is no reason that any force or violence shouldbe offered vnto vs. If it be the pleasure of Superiour powers to take away *Arimadono* his estate from him because we be Christians, we shall be very sory for it, but haue no fault at all therein, for we cannot put in hazard the saluation of our soules, which is for euer to endure, for an estate or life that is so short and brittle, and so soone to haue an end as this.

5. Notwithstanding this answere *Safioye* commanded them they should go and consult better vpon the matter among themselues, and after they had well considered, they should resolue what best they thought to do, and declare playnely whether they would obey vnto the *Xogun* or no, and leaue this obstinate cleauing vnto this new religion which the Fathers teach and preach.

6. In *Cuchinotzu* which is not far
from

from thence, the Christians (who be very anciét euer since the time of *Father Cosmo de Torres* companion of the Blessed *Father Xauier*) made the same preparation, and oathes among themselues that the others had done. *Safioye* vnderstanding thereof, sent for fiue of the chiefest and made vnto them a speach like to that which he made vnto the others although something more vehement and with greater promises : and they gaue him the same answere that the Christians of *Arima* before had done, and that many yeares ago they had made their resolution.

7. *Safuye* was much offended with their constancy and sayd, that seeing they were so obstinate in their opinion that he would giue notice thereof vnto the *Xogun*, and that without all doubt if they did not obey, *Arimadono* would loose his estate, they be tormented cruelly, and their wiues and children made slaues. For the *Xogun* would haue his will whatsoeuer came of it. *We should be*
glad

glad (ſayd they) *wee could conſerue* Arimadono *his eſtate with our goodes and liues,*
but if it cannot be otherwiſe done but by de-
nying of our Fayth, wee cannot de it, and
willing we ſhall bee to looſe all wee haue for
Chriſt, and for the ſaluation of our ſoules.
As for obeyng the Xogun, *we will do it wil-*
lingly in all thinges that do not concerne
our Fayth.

8. Theſe fiue being returned to *Cu-*
chinotzu, the feruour of the Chriſtians
there increaſed ſo much, that whereas
before there were but an 100. in the Cō-
fraternity, now there entred therin 400.
more, all of them making proteſtation
to dy for their religion, yea ſome Gentills
alſo moued with their example were
baptized with the ſame purpoſe and deſire: and many Chriſtians which before
had ſhewed themſelues but frayle and
weake, were thereby confirmed and reduced to the fayth.

9. *Safioye* went ſoone after to *Nan-*
gaſaqui, and from thence he wrot vnto
the *Xogun* how thinges paſſed in *Arima*:
whereupon

whereupon not longe after there came order from him , that *Arimadono* should go vnto the Kingdome of *Fiunga*, which was but bad newes for him. For whereas he hoped with the forsayd deuiles to haue gotten a better Eftate then that which he had before, now he found that it fell out cleane otherwile (and it was Godes punifhment vpon him for his cruelty againft the Chriftians) for he loft his old eftate which was very good , and the fubiects thereof very trufty and faythfull vnto him , and that which was giuen him was nothing fo but very dan-gerous, and euen in the middeft of all his enemies .

10.   This change and the many mif-fortunes which happened vnto him in his iorney both by fea and land , loofing fome fhipps with a great quantity of his goodes , and fome of his feruantes alfo (thofe only that were Gentills perifhing, and thofe that were Chriftians efcaping) encouraged them very much , feeing how manifeftly God Almighty began

to

to punish his Infidelity, and that the meanes which he tooke to conserue his estate, was the principall to ouerthrow it: and that he by whose counsell he had done so great mischiefe and wickednes (to wit *Safioyedono*) should be the man that wrought his vtter vndoing and perdition.

11. The Kingdome of *Biyen* and a good part of that of *Bungo* doth at the present belong to *Nangaou Yetchudono* one of the most noble and wise Princes of *Iapone*, who although a Gentill, yet was very well affected to the Fathers of the Society, to whome he and his sonne *Naiquidono* gaue a house and scituation many yeares ago in their Citties of *Conzura* and *Nagatzu*, & also leaue to preach and make as many Christians as they could, by which meanes there were many noble Christians in his Kingdōs. He was many tymes himselfe very neere being a Christian at the perswasion of *Don Iusto* whose most inward freind he was. And although he was not so happy

as

as to obteyne it , yet his wife *Dona Gratia*
did, as maybe seene in the 9. *Chap.* of the
second booke of the History of *Iapone*.
This Lady who was the daughter of *Cor-
eco Aquehi*, a great Lord that killed the
famous *Nobunanga*, was very wise and
of an excellent wit , and desired very
much to heare the reasons and grounds
of Christian Religiō , much moued therto with that which her husband *Yetchudono* had related vnto her thereof ; but it
was impossible that any man should get
into her pallace , nor for her to go out to
that effect , by reason that the noble La-
dyes of *Iapone* be very closely kept in , &
her husband was more rigorous in this
point then any other .

12 . Yet so it happened afterward
that *Taycosama* togeather with her husband and all the Princes of *Iapone* being
in the warres of *Satzuma* , in the yeare
1587 . she found meanes to go out of her
house to see the Temples of the Gentills
of *Ozaca*, and from thence she went secretly and disguised with many of her
women

women to the Church of the Fathers of the Society that was in that Citty. She tooke great pleasure, and particuler con-tentment to see it : and asking many doubtes and questions by meanes of her seruantes (because she would not disco-uer her selfe) about the Sects of *Iapone*, & concerning Christian religion, she not only remayned very well satisfied, but also exceeding desirous to heare the ser-mons of the Catechisme : and because she had no other meanes, she sent euery day some of the best intelligent & more ancient of her women vnto the Church, who hearing the Sermons did relate the vnto her in the best manner that they could. All the doubtes, difficulties, & arguments that offered themselues vnto her against those thinges of Christian religion she heard, she put downe still in writing to know the solution therof, and being fully satisfied at length in all matters, God Almighty giuing her an extraordinary light in the mysteries of our fayth, she was baptized by a Christi-

Q an

an Gentlewoman (becaufe it could not poffibly be done otherwife) that attended vpon her, with wonderous contentment to her foule, great aboundance of deuotion, and extraordinary plenty of comfortable teares. And although fhe neuer had any Prieft or other religious perfon to giue her inftructions, yet did God Almighty togeather with her Name communicate fpeciall grace vnto her: Her deuotion, patience, and humylity, was extraordinary, euidently appearing in all her actions, and feene in her letters and meffages.

13. To the end fhe might write vpon occafion vnto the Fathers about her foules affayres, and vnderftand their letters, fhe fecretly learned without the teaching of any both to read and writ after our manner of *Europe*, much differing from theirs. She caufed fome of her Children alfo to be baptized, and fifteene or more of her women and maydes, for which fhe receaued fom vnkindnes at her husbands hands: who yet when after her

death

death he came to know that she both liued and dyed a Christian (although he
neuer knew the manner of her conuersion) he shewed therefore great fauour
alwaies vnto the Fathers, and euery
yeare did cause her aniuersary funeralls
to be celebrated. And although he were
much molested by the *Xogun* and his Fauorites, and of the *Bonzi*, who neuer
left intreating him to haue no Churches
nor the Fathers in his Country: yet neuer was he moued, nor would giue any
eare vnto them, vntill the yeare 1611. in
which *Father Gregory Cespules* whome he
loued and esteemed very much departed
out of this life. For then vpon his death
he tooke occasion to deliuer himselfe
from the importunities of the *Xogun* &
his fauorites, and so he then wished the
Fathers that they would go vnto *Nanga-*
saqui, whither he sent vnto thē the wood
of their Houses and Churches, not doing
the least hurt or domage in the world vnto any of the Christians.

14.   When in the yeare 1614. he

vnderstood how *Don Iusto* his great freind had left and lost his estate for his fayth & religion he comended him very much for it , and said : If *Don Iusto* had not done in this occasion as he hath done, he should haue blemished all the noble actions of his life. For a magnanimous man both in prosperity and aduersity ought still to be the same without any chang or mutation at all.

15 . He sent diuers tymes vnto *Nangasaqui* to visit him: and vnto a Father of the Society with whome he was acquainted , he signified that he was very sory for the *Xoguns* manner of proceedinges : and that Father sending vnto him a treatise in which were answered the false calumniatiōs made against the Christian religion by the enemies thereof, he answered that he was well satisfied of all those thinges , but that it was necessary to haue patience for a tyme. Notwithstanding all this to giue contentment to the *Xogun*, he commanded that in his Country the common people
should

should be examined as they were in o-
ther places , among which there were
some that shewed not such constancy as
they ought to haue done . Amongst the
Gentlemē also there were diuers whome
he tempted & proued oftentymes to see
if they were truly firme and constant in
their fayth , or no , and they were of the
very principall about him , and such
as were in greatest fauour with him , for
he tooke great content to be serued and
accompanied with men of valour and
constancy, as indeed they were: for they
did plainely signify vnto his greatest fa-
uorite, to the end that it might come to
his notice , that the first tyme their Lord
did send a Message vnto them to leaue
their fayth and religion,he should ioyntly therewithall send some that might cut
off their heades , or put them to some o-
ther death,for that they were not willing
to shew themselues discourteous vnto
him , as it might be they might seeme , if
they came to be questioned about their
religion , for the which they were reso-
Q 3
lued

ued to suffer any thing, yea and finally
to spend their bloud and giue vp their
liues.

Of the Glorious Death of Adam Aracaua,
and of the Christians of Xiqui, *and*
Conzura.

CHAP. XII.

THE Ilandes of *Xiqui,* or *Amacusa*
and *Conzura,* are part of the
Kingdome of *Fingo.* They did
first belong vnto *Don Augustino Tzuno
Camidono,* in whose tyme all the Inhabitants thereof were Christians, baptized
by the Fathers of the Society: but after
his death which was in the yeare 1600.
they were giuen vnto *Ximadono,* who put
therein certaine Gouernours, who although Gentills, yet did they shew much
fauour vnto the Fathers, who vsed to
visit them now and then, for the keeping and conseruing thereof.

2.   When the newes of this persecution

tion came vnto *Ximadono*, he being then
in the Kingdome of *Fixen*, where commonly he makes his aboad, he wrote
presently vnto the Fathers, that he was
verysoryto heare of that new order made
by the *Xogun*, but that he could not
choose but be obedient thereunto, and
that therefore he desired they would depart his country vntill they saw what
would be the end thereof.

3 . Hereupon they al departed soone
after to the griefe of the Christians, yea
and of the Gentills also who did loue
them very much. But because the Christians should not remayne without all
comfort, although none of the Fathers
could remayne amongst them, yet did
they leaue with them a good old man
called *Adám*, who was the Porter of their
house, and because he had a sonne that
dwelt there in the towne of *Xiqui*, could
with better colour stay. In *Conzura* also
there stayed another whose name was
Soter, of whose glorious Martyrdome
mention shall be made in the 9. Chapter
of

of the second part of this relation.

4.   *Ximadono* sent word vnto his Gouernours that he went vnto the Court,
and that from thence he would write
what should be done with the Christias:
but being in the way aduertised how ri-
goroufly they were dealt withall in *Meaco*, he wrote againe vnto *Xiroyemondono*
his principall gouernor of those Ilandes,
and to the reft, that they should not leaue
one Christian in them vnder paine of
loofing their eftates, yea and their liues
alfo, for that the *Xogun* had fo commanded it. The Gouernour vfed great diligence in the bufines, and after fome tyme
fignified vnto *Ximadono*, that there were
now no Chriftians in the Ilands, which
he did (it being moft falfe) becaufe he
bare no hatred but rather good affection
towardes them, & thought therby to co-
ply fufficiently with the *Xogun*, to whofe
command they would feeme to haue o-
beyed for feare of incurring his difgrace.

5.   *Adam* the good old man in the
meane

meane tyme went vp and downe viſi-
ting the Chriſtians in their howſes , and
animating them. The Gouernour hauing
intelligence thereof , gaue command he
ſhould be taken , & that diligence ſhould
be vſed to perſwade him to forſake his
Fayth . He hearing of it , lifted vp his
handes to heauen , gaue many thankes ro
God , and would not abſent himſelte as
ſome aduiſed him , but went directly to
his ſones houſe , there to expect the combat , hoping for it afterwards to haue a
crowne in heauen . Thither came many
Gētills that were his freinds , to perſwade
him al they could , but he with corage of
mind did aſwere them in this māner. *Are
you not aſhamed to perſwade me to ſo baſe
a thinge for a man of my age , and that haue
beene ſo many yeares a Chriſtian ? Although
it were only for worldly reſpect, I cannot now
go backe , hauing ſerued the Fathers ſo many
yeares , & receaued ſo many benefitts at their
handes: and I do remayne heere to do my beſt
endeauour that the reſt of the Chriſtians remayne conſtant in their faith , how cā I leaue*
Q 5　　　　　　　　　　　　　　*it*

it my selfe ? Tell them that sent you , and set
you on worke , that in this only busines I must
neyther regard the Gouernour , nor Ximadono , nor the Xogun himselfe , but only God
Almighty , who is my Lord and Sauiour .

6.   The same perswasions were made
him by all the officers , but he being nothing at all moued there with , nor seeming much to regard them , they tooke
and carried him prisoner vnto the Castle
vpō the Thursday before the holy Week,
wherewith he seemed exceeding glad ,
because he said it was so neere the tyme
of the passion of his Sauiour and Redeemer . The Gouernour commanded that
they should put him all that night in the
prison , and in some paine , to see if therewithall he would be brought to change
his determination : but seeing in the
morning no change at all in him , he sent
for him , & in presence of other Gentills
he sayd vnto him : *Adam* , you knowe
well inough the great loue that I alwaies
did beare vnto the Fathers , and that I
beare no euill will vnto your religion:
but

but it is the *Xoguns* command, and *Xi-uadono* hath signified vnto me, that he
will make me be put to death, if I suffer
so much as one only Christian to remayne in his Country: let me intreat
you therefore you would dissemble a
little for the present, and not to go animating the rest.

7. *Of your loue to the Fathers* (said
Adam) *I am a good witnesse, and they I
know will neuer cease to be thankefull for it.
But in this matter, seeing it is a thing that
doth concerne the saluation of my soule, I
cannot bee obedient to you therein. Your
worship sayth, that you persecute the Christiãs
against your will, only because you would not
loose your estate and life; and I because I
would not loose the estate of euerlasting life
am determined to perseuer vnto death in the
faith of Christ. If I for obeying you should
be damned to the eternall torments of hell
fire, neyther your Worship, nor the* Xogun
*with al his power could deliuer me from them;
& although yee could, yet haue I receaued so
many benefites of my Lord & Sauiour Iesus
Christ,*

Chrift , that I cannot without moft bafe in-
gratitude comit fo vile an act , as to leaue his
fayth . Your Worfhip therefore may do with
me as you pleafe , for neyther will i my felfe
leaue my religion, nor yet perfwade any other
to do it .

8.   The Gouernour being much o-
ffended with this anfwere , commanded
him to be ftripped naked : and the good
old man glad to fee fo good a beginning,
and giuing thankes to Almighty God for
it, did help himfelfe to pul of his cloaths,
which being done they bound him with
cordes , and carried him in that manner
through the ftreets to his publique fhame
commanding that all fhould come out of
their houfes to looke & gaze vpon him ,
which being done they left him bound
in the ftreet vntil fuch tyme as they had
fet vp two thick poftes ech of them of
a fadom high diftant foure or fiue hand-
breadths one from the other , and put
another peece of wood through them
both , and aboue it a rope . To thefe two
poftes they tyed his handes and feet
in

in forme of a Croffe with fo great rigour that the tops of his toes did fcarce touch the ground. In this manner he remayned from Friday before Palme funday vntill holy Saturday with was Eafter Eue, although leaft he fhould dy with the torment thereof, and the Chriftians reuerence him as a Martyr, they tooke him thence in the night tyme, as alfo when it rayned or fnowed more thē ordinary. It was a ftrange thing that he being 63 . yeares old & newly recouered of a great ficknefle, though he ftood there naked all that tyme expofed to the cold which was exceeding great, yet did he neuer make any fhew or figne of feeling any greife at all.

9. A Father of the Society that had beene banifhed from thence, and was now retourned againe fecretly, to vifit the Chriftians, fent vnto him to animate him in his tormentes, and he anfwered. *Tell the Father that I am of very good courage, defire him to commend me vnto God in his prayers, and that fince I haue beene put*
here

heere in this torment I felt nothing at all of my sicknes and infirmity. Many and great perswasions were vsed vnto him all this tyme . One sayd vnto him : *Adam,* verily I cannot imagine in what you put your hope to be so obstinate, for it is reported as most certaine that neither any Church shall stand, nor Father stay in all *Iapone . If my hope said he were placed in these things your newes would trouble me, suppose they were certaine, as I thinke they be not : but it is not placed in them, but in Almighty God who is in all places, and not subiect to mutation : and I hope in him that if they do cast downe the Churches, and banish the Fathers; yet will he when it pleaseth him, build them vp a new, and bring the Fathers backe a gaine to* Iapone . *Of this good Lord I hope to haue strength to endure my toments, and to perseuer vnto the end, and afterwards to be bountifully rewarded by him for it .*

10. When they were most busy with him to perswade him, he looked still to heauen, and offered vp his prayers : and it seemed that sometymes he was as it
were

were in extaſy, the very poſition of his
body much mouing thoſe that beheld
him to deuotion. He was bound in the
manner of a S . *Andrews* Croſſe, and his
armes being tyed by the elbowes, hee
lifted vp his handes (togeather with his
eyes) to heauen, but could not make thē
to meet. He ſpake vnto the Chriſtians
ſtill with great loue and affection, animating them, and deſiring them to pray
for him vnto God. If they asked of him
that he would pray for them in heauen,
he did humble himſelfe ſaying, *that he
was a ſinner & not worthy of ſo great a good.*
After this they carried him vnto another
place that was both more publique and
more cold, with intention to diſgrace &
torment him more. But he ſtill remained the ſame man, without any change
at all. Vpon holy Saturday or Eaſter eue,
becauſe they feared the Chriſtiãs would
be to much encouraged with his exãple,
they looſed him from the tormenting
place, and put him in the houſe of a
Chriſtian, a freind of his, who did enter
into

into band to deliuer him whenſoeuer
they ſhould aske for him , & ſo he ſtaied
in that houſe two monthes without any
keeper at all .

11.   Three other Chriſtians were
tyed at the ſame time , and in the ſame
place with *Adam* , but they were not
ſtripped naked as he was , nor yet ſtayed
ſo long in the torment as he did , for that
their kinred and freinds did promiſe the
Gouernour that they would make them
deny their fayth , although vnto them
they ſayd nothing els , but only that they
had obteined licence for them to liue as
Chriſtians . The Gouernour was much
delighted with this deceitfull deuiſe , &
greatly deſired the ſame tricke might
be put vpon *Adam:* but he was ſo careful
of himſelfe that they could not poſſibly
do it .

12.   The two monethes he remayned in his freindes houſe after he was
taken from the torment , he liued a moſt
holy life , ſpending all his tyme in a little
Chamber there about a fadome ſquare ,
                                    eyther

eyther talking with the Christians, that came thither, of spirituall matters, or els in prayer or reading the booke of the imitation of Christ. He neuer went out from thence vnlesse it were in the night to bury some dead body. With the Gentills that came with purpose to peruert him he vsed such kind of speaches and behauiour, that they did not long molest and trouble him. The Gouernour sent him word that he was determined to cause his fingers and his toes to be cut off, not in that manner that the payne thereof should make him dye, as he desired to do, but one by one, at seuerall tymes and dayes, to torment him therewith the more : to which he answered : *I am ready, willing, and prepared to suffer those tormentes you speake of and greater to, & I hope in God that he wil giue me strength for all. If I dy in them, my lot shall be the happier, and my ioy the greater : and if not, yet to haue suffered them will be some satisfaction for my sinnes. Only this I desire, that if it be resolued on as you say it is, that they would*

R   *begin*

begin to execute it presently, for being an old.
man as I am, I do desire before I dye to haue
some part of the merit.

13. The Gouernour with this answere was astonished, & in a rage commanded that they should begin the execution of it presently. But his man fearing some punishment from heauen if so
cruell a torment should haue beene inflicted vpon the innocent & holy man,
he caused it to be differred vntil another
tyme. After that *Adam* had giuen this
answere vnto the Gouernour he felt in
himselfe extraordinary ioy, with many
heauenly comfortes and celestiall consolations. And as he tould a certaine
friend of his in great secrecy, he saw one
tyme our Blessed Lady the most happy
mother of our Sauiour Christ with a
Crosse in her hand, by which he vnderstood that he should obtayne the glorious Crowne of Martyrdome. And
whereas before this tyme he could not
endure to heare others say that he should
be a Martyr, holding himselfe for vnworthy

worthy thereof : euer after this he delighted very much to heare and speake
of it. That he had other heauenly visi-
ons besides this, might be also gathered
by his wordes, though through humility
he neuer would declare them vnto any.

14.   The Gouernour afterwardes
vfed meanes that *Adam* might secretly
escape, and go vnto *Nangasaqui*, and he
hauing notice thereof said : *What fly ? in*
no case I . If they will banish me, giuing me a
note vnder their handes, that hauing so long
tyme perswaded me that I should leaue the
fayth of Christ, yet I would not, and that
therefore they do banish me, then will I goe,
and not otherwise.

15.   The Gouernour durst not giue
him such a note, but differred the sentence which was giuen of cutting of his
toes and fingers by little and little, carrying him naked through all the Ilandes
for an example to all Christians vntill he
had consulted the matter with the rest of
Ximadono his Gouernours : which when
he had done, and had related vnto them

the whole discourse, they all answered, that it would be a great discredit both vnto him and *Ximadono* allo, if so rebellious and obstinate a fellow as they termed him, were not seuerely punished: that the sentence of death should be notified vnto him, and if he did not change his minde, also executed. Hereupon immediatly they notified vnto *Adam* the sentence, wherwith he receiued no small comfort. And it being published in the Country thereaboutes, there came thither so great a multitude of Christians to be present at his martyrdome, that they durst not put him to death publiquely, least they should take his body for reliques. They caried him therefore bound vnto the Castle, giuing out that his death should be very publique after some foure or fiue dayes.

16. The Christians vsed all meanes possible, for some of them at the least, to haue beene present at his death: but it could not be, for one night very secretly they tooke him out of the Castle and

carried

carried him to the place of Martyrdome,
whither he went with great ioy and
alacrity, although the way was very
rugged, and the night exceeding darke,
and they had no torches nor other light
at all, becaufe of going with more fe-
crecy: and whereas fome of the company
ftumbled almoft at euery ftep, yet did he
go with fuch agility and nimblenes, that
he was euer the foremoft of them all.
Being come vnto the place he kneeled
downe vpon his knees, prayed moft deuoutly, and at two blowes had his head
ftroken off. For it being fo darke a night
that the executioner could not fee, he
gaue the firft blow vpon his fhoulders,
at the which he neuer fo much as moued,
but quietly expected the fecond, twice
inuoking aloud the bleffed name of *Iefus.*
And the Gentills themfelues did teftify
that after his head was fallen downe v-
pon the ground, he named twice more
that moft holy Name, fo loud, that it
might haue beene heard through all the
valley, whereat they wondering faid:

R 3

That

That only to haue seene the constancy and ioy wherewithall Adam dyed, were motiue i-nough to moue any man to be a Christian: & that it was no: possible, but that one dying so as he did should be saued.

17. They tooke his holy body and trayled it vnto the Sea shoare, and there wrapping it togeather with his head in a net, tying stones vnto it to make it sinke, they cast it into the Sea, because the Christians should not find it, & so reuerence any of his reliques.

18. Though this Martyrdome were done so secretly, as I haue said, yet did the Christians suspect it, and thereupon some of them went vnto the place where it was done, but they found there only some little quantity of his fresh bloud, the which with part of his apparel they tooke with great deuotion, and returned with all speed possible, because the Gentills were now comming backe againe thither to couer the bloud, to the end no signe at all should remaine of his Martyrdome. The Christians of *Xiqui*,

and

and other places vsed great diligence
with nets and hooks, and other instru-
mentes to haue found and taken vp his
holy body : and there was a Spaniard
that offered 500. Ducates to any one
that could bring it him, but it could not
possibly be found.

19. Diuers Christians did affirme,
that for many dayes togeather there was
seene a great brightnes ouer the place
where this holy seruant of God was put
to death, as also ouer that place of the
Sea wherein his body was cast, the
which is so certaine, so many Christians
seeing it altogether, sometymes fourty,
soetymes fifty, sometymes more, not once
nor twice but often tymes, that there
can be made no doubt thereof. Some
there were that would not beleeue it because themselues did not see it with the
rest, which yet afterwardes hauing dis-
posed themselues by prayer to that end,
did most cleerly & euidently see and perceiue it.

20. Many notable thinges might be
related

R 4

related of this holy man, but omitting all
the reſt I will only ſet downe two which
in my opinion ſeeme very worthy of memory. An ancient Chriſtian thinking
in his hart within himſelfe what tormentes might be giuē him which might
make him wauer in the profeſſion of his
faith, and all ſeeming very eaſy to him
to endure, only the thought that ſeauen
younge Children which he had ſhould
be tormented before his face, and that
his wife ſhould be carried through the
ſtreets to publique ſhame, did terrify him
exceeding much, and make him ſomewhat wauer in his mind. All this paſſed
in his hart within himſelfe, not ſpeak-
ing of it one word at all to any one aliue.
This man afterwards went to viſit *Adam*
when he was in priſon, who ſeeing him
ſaid: *What an impreſſion did the imaginatiō
of your wiues publique ſhame, and your Childrens tormenting make in you? O what a deceipt is this! Be not afrayd, for he that giues
courage for one thinge will giue alſo for the
reſt.* The man was aſtoniſhed when he
perceaued

perceaued that *Adam* had feene and vnderftood that which he only thought
within himfelfe, and was encouraged
thereby to confeffe his faith, and fuffer
for it all that fhould be offered.

21.   Another man being ouercome
by faire words and intreaties, did fhew
fome frailty in the confeffion of his
fayth, who going afterwardes to vifit
Adam, he reprehended him very fharply
for it, but after he was gone from thence
Adam faid vnto thofe that were prefent :
*This man being importunated did fhew fome
frailty, but he will ftoutly ftand heereafter
for the honour of God*. And fo it happened
indeed, for he repenting himfelfe of his
fault, and very fory for it, went to one
of the Officers who had beene the occafion of his finne, and in his houfe in the
prefence of diuers Gentills faid vnto
him : *Sir you remember well the meanes you
vfed with me to make me leaue the faith of
Chrift, and I moued with your intreaties did
fhew my felfe vnconftant and cowardly : But
in very truth did not leaue to be a Chriftian,*

R 5   *nor*

nor to say my beades : and now euery night I do discipline my selfe for the sinne I then comitted. I do desire you very earnestly you would hould me for a Christian, and to signify the same to all that haue had notice of my fall.

22. The Gentill was much offended to heare him speake in that manner, as also the rest that were present, saying, that, that which he desired could neither be granted nor permitted being contrary to the *Xoguns* comand. To which he replying, that at least they would let him haue his beades and pictures publiquely: they being very angry thrust him out of the roome disgracfully, with many threatning speaches. But he to shew that he neither was affraid of them, nor ashamed to be accounted a Christan, went imediatly into the Kitchen of the house, and taking vp a hoat burning Iron that was there, he made therewith a great Crosse in his forehead, burning his flesh exceedingly, and so returning to the place where the Gentills were, he said vnto the:

My

My Maisters now that I haue made this sign
of the holy Crosse in my forehead, no man
can doubt but that I am a Christian: well
may you giue me all the torments that you
please, for I hope in God since he hath giuen
me strength to do this, he will also giue me
courage to suffer whatsoever else.

23. The Gouernour afterward had
notice of this action, and determined to
haue punished him seuerely for it, but
others disswaded him saying, that with
the example of *Adam* and of this man
there would be many more that would
offer themselues to martyrdome, if he
did deale any further therein. Whereupon he dissembled the matter, and the
good Christian who remained marked
for al his life, did say that after he heard
Adams words he could neuer be quiet in
mind vntill he had made this Confessiō
of his Fayth, and with his example ani-
mated all the other Chistians to be constant and couragious.

24. The Fathers of the Society
were also banished out of the Country
of

of *Cenzura*, although the Gouernour
there was not so rigorous in his proceedings as in some other places, for that
he did not imediatly set vpon the Christians, but after some tyme, and that only to make a shew that he had some respect vnto the *Xoguns* order. He commanded first of all, six good Christians
who had the care and custody of six
Churches committed vnto them, as also
to animate the rest of the Christians in
the Fathers absence to depart the Country: then he banished eleuen or twelue
ouer Christians that had beene banished
out of other kingdomes for their fayth,
and were retyred thither to haue meanes
to liue neere to the Church: so that one
with another there were banished out of
that Country some two hundred and
fifty Christians, all very ioyfull and content to see themselues so often banished,
so tossed and turmoyled for the fayth of
Christ.

25. After this they gaue out that
they would carry all the women, that
would

would not leaue to be Christians,
through all the townes naked to their
publike shame; the which did cause in
them all great feare and trouble. But one
among the rest, a woman of good estate,
did animate them all, saying : *That it*
were not much for them to passe that shame
for Christ, seeing he had suffered the same
for them, and that she was ready and prepa-
red to be carried so through all the townes
and Citties of Iapone, rather then once to
offend Almighty God. With this the rest
were much encouraged, and so they seeing the Gouernour comming a little after into the streetes with armed men, all
of them that could did go together to one
place animating one another to dye for
their Religion. But the gentills meaning
only to make a demonstration that they
did obey the *Xoguns* Command, and to
haue some colour afterwardes to giue out
that now there were no Christians in
the Country, they went only vnto some
few poore persons that were without the
towne, & perswading them to subscribe
according

according to their pleafure, they returned with great triumph, publifhing a-
broad that now all had left the profeffion of the Chriftian fayth. Whereupon
they caft downe the Churches, and cut
downe all the Croffes; but the Chriftians fet vp one again on a mountaine not
farr of from the towne, whither they
went to pray at fundry tymes, and do
their difciplines. The like happened to
the Chriftians of *Oyano*, which is another
Iland neere adioyning thereto, fome of
them being very much abufed, others
banifhed for their fayth.

*Of that which paffed in other places: And
of the glorious death of Minalius in
Fucofoti.*

CHAP. XIII.

HAVINGE related that which
happened in other Kingdomes,
it remayneth now that we fpeak
a little of fuch thinges as paffed at this
tyme

tyme in the Citty of *Nangasaqui*, and in
other townes neere adioyning thereto.
The Fathers of the Society had fiue or
six Houses in the Kingdome of *Fixen*,
besides those which they had in *Nangasaqui*, and besides diuers other Chappells
which they often visited. The first was
in *Isafay*, where the Lord or Prince although a Gentill being a freind vnto
thē, did desire to conserue the Churches
and Christians in peace and quietnes :
yet for feare of the *Xogun*, he comanded
first that the Church of *Isafay* should be
taken downe, leauing the other houses
standing as they were, and that the
Churches of the villages should be so
disguised that they should not seeme to
be that which they were : yet he permitted a Father to come and visit the Christians secretly. A little after this he made
a Proclamation, in which he did command that all should leaue to be Christians, as the *Xogun* had ordained, but yet
vnder hand he gaue order that in the exe-
cutiō, no rigour should be vsed, although
                                    some

fome Noble men his fubiectes moued
eyther with hatred towards the Chriftian faith, or with that they faw practifed
in other places, did very much perfecute
their feruantes, who thereby manifefted
their Conftancy, and defire to dy for
their Religion, fome of them fuffering
banifhment, and loofing therby al that
which they had, others being ready to
do the fame, were permitted for a tyme
and winked at.

2.   The Fathers had another howfe
in *Fudoyama*, from whence they did vfe
to vifit part of the eftate of *Omura* and
other Territories thereabout. The *Bonzi*
of *Omura* did make earneft fuite vnto the
Prince, that he would compell his fubiectes to imbrace their fect, and leaue the
faith of Chrift : but he made anfwere
vnto them, that for religio̅ fake he would
not depriue himfelfe of his ancient fubiectes ; telling them moreouer, that if
they were fo certaine that their fect was
good and true, they fhould conuince the
Chriftians with their reafons, and not
                                   compell

compell them by force . Yet notwithstanding to giue them some content , he
made a law that whosoeuer did receaue
any of the Fathers into his house should
incurre the forfeyture of a certaine some
of money , but they for all that neyther
left to intertaine them , nor yet to seeke
and make inquiry after them . *Ximadano*
vsed more extremity , for that he seized
vpon the goodes and landes of the Christians of *Caratzu* , banishing them out
of his Countries . And one among the
rest who in that occasion left all he had
with great courage and content was
George Acasioye , of whose notable feruour and glorious death we shall make
mention in the 10. Chapter of the second Part of this narration. *Nabexima-
dono* , who was the Prince of that country , gaue comand , that the Church of
Fundyima should be pulled downe , but
towardes the Christians no rigour at all
was vsed ; & so one of the Fathers did remayne there secretly & visited them al of-
tetyms , with no lesse labour then content.

3. In this Countrey there was a Christian to whose care the keeping was committed of a Church and the thinges therein, and certaine Gentills intending by force to take a picture out of it, he tould them couragiously, that he would sooner loose his head, then let it go. They durst not kill him without order from the Prince, who at that tyme was farr off, & on the other syde they feared least he would fly away before the answere came. The which when he vnderstood he bouldly went vnto them, and said. *Go aske the Prince what his pleasure is to haue done with me, and I will stay here till you returne. If I fly you shall vnderstand thereby that I leaue to be a Christian, which is that which you desire.* There he remayned expecting a good while; at length the sentence came that they should take all he had from him, and put him out of the Country, and so it was put in execution, and he taking with him the picture went to *Nangasaqui* more contented in his owne mind, then if he had carried with him

him all his wealth , and much more then that he had before.

4. The third & fourth houſes which the Fathers had in this Kingdome were in *Vracami*, and *Mongui*, in which places becauſe they were ſo neere to *Nangaſaqui* there was no other thing done , but on-ly preparations made for the generall aſſault which all did expect would ſoone after follow. Their fifth Houſe was in *Fucafori*, where there was more copious and glorious fruit . This towne is ſubiect to the Lord of *Fixen*, and ſtandeth at the entrance of the Port or Hauen of *Nangaſaqui*. When *Safioyedono* was made Gouernor of *Nangaſaqui*, he being very zealous in the ſuperſtitious religion of the Gentills, and hauing no place within the Citty where to vſe his Heatheniſh rites (all being there Chriſtians) he cauſed a little temple (which they call *Mia*) to be made in *Fucafori*, whither he went to that purpoſe as often as oc-caſion was required. It greeued him very much, to ſee a Church of the Chriſtians

S 2   there,

there, and he so continued the matter that
the yeare last past it was cast downe
without any other domage done vnto
the Christians : but now vpon this occasion he caused a Proclamation to be made
that all should leaue their fayth vnder
great paines & forfeytures : to the which
the Christians all with one accord answered, that although it cost them their
liues they would not do it. Whereupon
the Gouernour sending for the Chiefe
of them, gaue them very bad speaches,
calling them fooles & Asses, that wheras following the Sectes of *Iapone*, they
might saue their soules and ioyntly liue
in pleasure, prosperity, and content :
yet they would rather follow a hard Religion, taught only by a few strangers,
& that with danger to loose their goodes
and liues, and the liberty of their wiues
and Children.

5. To the which one of the Christians in name of the rest answered in
this manner : *My Lord, the reason why we
imbrace and follow the fayth of Christ ; is
becaufe*

because it is manifest vnto vs, that in it only
we can be saued and not in any of the sectes of
Iapone ,which be both very different and dis-
agreeing among themselues, and all of them
without any solid ground and true foundati-
on . And in matters concerning the gayning
or loosing of eternall life ,it were no wisdome,
but plaine folloy , to haue too much regard to
the losse of temporall goodes , as all thinges in
this world be . The Gouernour replyed,
asking him, If he had euer seen or spoken
with any post , or other messenger that
came from the other world, and brought
newes of another life . *The reasons my*
Lord (said he) *are so euident , that there*
is another life , and the testimonies and ar-
gumentes that our religion is the only truth,
are so strong, that they be of much more force
and efficacy then the wordes of any Messenger
in the world. If it please your Lordship to heare
the Sermons ,you shall easily see the truth .of
the Christian fayth , and euidently perceaue
the falsity of all the Sectes of Iapone . With
this the Gouernour growing into great
choler, commanded them imediatly to
deliuer

deliuer vp to him their Rofaries , to whõ
one named *Peter* anfwered very ftoutly .
There is none here will leaue his fayth or de-
liuer vp his Rofary , and if for this caufe you
will depriue vs of our liues,we are all ready &
prepared to giue them willingly. And with
that he went away . *Peter* his Father in
law,who was a Gentill,fearing left fome
hurt would come vnto him , for that
which he had fpoken , intreated the Gouernour to pardon him for that he was
but a yong man, and had fpoken rafhly
without mature confideration , and that
he would enter into bondes to make him
leaue his fayth .

6 .   *Peter* vnderftanding what his
Father in law had done and faid,prefent-
ly fent vnto him his wife and children
with this meffage. *The loue of your daugh-*
ter and grandchildren haue made you promife
for me , that which you ought not to haue
done : here therefore I fend you them , and I
without them fhall dy more freely , and with
more content . And vnto the Gouernour
he fent word , that he would not ftand

to

to that which his Father in law had pro
mised in his behalfe : and that moreouer
he was not sorry for the wordes which
he had spoken in his presence ; and because he did expect no lesse then to be
put to death for them, he therefore for
that effect sent him there is sword. But
the Gouernour dissembling the matter,
would not proceed any further against
him, contenting himselfe with his Father in law his word and promise, wher-
by *Peter* escaped death at that tyme, gayning notwithstanding doubtlesse for his
worthy resolution great merit at God
Almighty his handes.

7. At the same tyme, and vpon the
same occasion there were two brethren
named *Mine Cosmo*, and *Mine Luis*, who
answered very constantly that in no case
they would leaue the fayth of Christ,
the which for so many yeares they had
professed. And although the Gouernour
vsed all meanes possible to make them
condescend vnto his will, at least in outward shew, yet could he not moue them

S 4   any

any thing at all, they still resisting most
couragiously. He told them he was very
sorry that they being of his name, and
something also of kinred vnto him,
would cause him insteed of fauour to
proceed with rigour against them. They
answered, that they, their wiues & children were Christians, and by Godes
holy grace would so remaine, and that
for their holy religion they were ready
to giue their liues. Whereupon the Gouernour comanded them to keep their
owne house as a prison vntill he had consulted with the Prince what should be
done. Vpon this it seemed vnto them
that they were now in great liklihood to
obteine the crowne of Martirdōe which
they so much desired: the better therfore
to prepare themselues thereto they went
one night to *Nangasaqui*, and there confessed themselues, desiring the Fathers
to pray for them, that for their sinnes &
owne vnworthines they might not loose
their crowne which they expected. The
same night they returned home againe,
made

made themselues now apparell , and bought candles to carry in their handes when they should be carried to Martyrdome, expecting euery houre with great desire their iudgment, sentence and condemnation .

8. Vpon *Corpus Christi* day in the morning the Gouernour sent word vnto *Luis* , that he meant that day to go to recreate himselfe , and see some fishing in the Sea , and that he desired to haue him go with him to keep him company . *Luis* at the first thought to haue excused himselfe by reason it was so great a holy day, but afterwards vpon further consideration, surmysing what the matter might be , taking his leaue of all his family , he went with much alacrity , and the boat in which they went being now almost a league in the sea from the land , the Gouernour sayd vnto him : *Luis* do you remaine stil setled in the opinion you were of three dayes past in being and continuing still a Christian ? *Yes indeed do I* (said Luis) *and am very well content and*

S 5   *desirous*

desirous to dye for it . Thereupon all those
that were in the boat mocked and scof-
fed at him , as if he had beene a foole or
a madman : but he little regarded their
wordes, & seemed to be nothing moued
with their iniurious speaches: the which
the Gouernour perceiuing commanded
that his head should be cut of imediatly ,
the which was done at two blowes , he
being vpon his knees and most deuoutly
inuoking the holy name of Iesus . His
head being cut off they tyed stones ther-
unto, as also vnto his holy body, and cast
them both into the sea , because no reliques of him should remayne : returning
home they confiscated his goods & house
making his wife a slaue . The same they
did with the wife children and goods of
Cosmo his elder brother, whome they banished out of the country , the which he
accepted willingly being no lesse ioyfull
to loose that which he had for Christ, the
full of sorrow that he was not companion to his brother in the Crowne of
Martyrdome .

9 . The

9. The manner of *Luis* his Martyrdome being once known in *Nangasaqui*,
no diligence was left vndone to find his
holy body, being sought for by diuers
persons with all care and diligence for
fiue dayes togeather, but could not find
so much as the least signe thereof, although they knewe the place where it
was cast into the sea. Vpon the fifth day,
they saw a kind of cleere brightnes ouer
a certaine place, as those that found it
did affirme, and taking that for a signe
thereof, they sought there, and so found
it presently, & carried it vnto the Fathers
of the Society who did with al reuerence
place it in the Church of the *Misericordia*
with intention, heareafter when this
storme is past, to build a Church in *Fucafori* to the glory of God, in memory of
him.

Of

Of such thinges , as passed in Nangasaqui, *before the banishment .*

CHAP. XIIII.

THERE were in *Nangasaqui,* as I said in the 5 . Chapter , foure Churchs of the Society of Iesus, three Monasteries , of *S . Austin* , *S. Dominicke* , and *S . Francis* , foure Parish Churches, and three or foure Chappells All the inhabitantes thereof and of the country round about were Christians . There at this time were al the Fathers gathered together expecting eyther the execution of the sentence , giuen by the *Xogun* before mentioned of their finall banishment, or els perhaps some mitigation thereof, by meanes and mediation of the *Portugalls,* whose ships were shortly expected to come thither . In the same expectation were *Don Iusto* , *Don Iohn* , and the rest of those that were banished from the *Caini:* exceeding was the
concourse

concourse of Christians from all partes
of *Iapone* thither, some to take their leaue,
others to receaue the Sacraments therby
to arme themselues for the future fight ,
all lamenting the losse they were to su-
staine by the departure of their spirituall
maysters, pastors, guides, and ghostly
Fathers , and so great was their feruour ,
that vntil the end of October they scarce
euer let the Fathers rest neither by day
nor night, comming to them continually
for counsaile, comfort, direction and
aduise.

2 . At the beginning of this yeare
the Bishop of *Iapone* , *Don Luis Cerqueira*
of the Society of Iesus departed out of
this life . He was a man of great wisdom
and learning , and of no lesse vertue ,
piety , & sanctity of life, & very zealous
of the good of his Church , which by his
death at that tyme sustayned a wonderous losse . Greatly was he grieued to see
so cruell a persecution raysed against his
flocke, and that he could not by any
meanes remedy it , nor defend his sheep
from

from the cruell wolues . Some monthes
before the persecution did begin he fell.
sicke , and after with the newes thereof
and griefe ther at his sicknesse dayly did
increase , and so within a few dayes no
phisicke being of force to prolonge or
saue his life, he gaue his soule vnto Alm.
God , vnto whose paternall prouidence
he did commend his poore afflicted
Church , desiring him eyther to defend
and succour it , or els to giue force and
strength to the Christians to suffer and
endure the violent and tyranicall proceedinges of the Gentills their enemies a-
gainst them . His death was vpon the
16. of February 1614 .

3 . Sixetene yeares had he gouerned
that new planted Church with great re-
ctitude and rare examplar life , and in
that tyme he had seene many different
successes, sometimes great prosperity in
the conuersion of many soules and men
of worth , vnto the fayth of Christ : at
other tymes great aduersities , afflictions
and persecutions, in all which he alwaies
                                                   shewed

shewed a great quietnes and serenity of mind , and a firme trust and confidence in God. He was much respected and beloued of his flock, & of all the religious persons that were in *Iapone*: yea the *Xogun* himselfe, his Courtiers and Fauorites when some yeares agoe he did visit them, did commend and esteeme him very much ; so did likewise all the Lordes and Princes , though they were otherwise, as Gentills, not affected to religion : for which reason at this tyme there was great want of him , and his death was much lamented generally of all .

4. After his death Father Prouinciall of the Society remayned with the care of the gouernement of the Bishopricke , vntil such tyme as another Pastor should be appointed, and for that respect, as also for the obligation of the common good of all the Christians of *Iapone* , he determined with the aduice and counsaile of the rest of the religious, to send vnto the Court-Father *Iames Mesquita* of the
Society

Society, who had beene a long tyme
Rector of the Colledg of *Nangasaqui*, &
was well acquainted with the *Safioye*,
to deale with the *Xogun*, and to giue him
information of the truth of all matters.
The Father went and did his best endeauours, but the *Safioye* himselfe being the
Chiefe sticler in the busines, gaue him
answere, that it was not possible to haue
audience in that matter, because the *Xogun* was already fully resolued that not
so much as one of all the Fathers should
remayne in all the Country, and therewith he comanded him imediatly to returne to *Ningasaqui*, where all did prepare themselues to the conflict no lesse
then in other places, vsing to that end al
spirituall meanes they could, now that
there was no hope in humane diligence.

5.   In the Colledge of the Society
comonly there were wont to be before
this persecution began foure thousand
Comunicants, and more in euery of the
principall feastes of the yeare; but now
there was much greater concourse both
of

of those that dwelt within the Citty, as
also of those that came from abroad and
liued in other places. Scarce were there
any that did not make in this occasion a
general confession of al their life,thereby
to prepare themselues the better to Martyrdome : many both men and women
made themselues new clothes, therein
to signify the gladnes and willingnes of
their mindes to suffer death, or any tormentes for their faith, as also to receiue
them therein with more decency. To the
end that al might be holpen and sufficiently instructed in this occasion, & this
doe with the least note possible, was appointed in euery street one house where
the people commonly met togeather to
make the prayer of Fortie-howres, six
or seauen Preachers going out of the
Colledge euery day thither to make them
exhortations, and instruct them how
they ought to behaue themselues in the
confession of their faith, in their tormentes,and in Martyrdome it selfe : and
in these places inumerable were the prai-

T   ers,

ers, fastes, disciplines, and other pennances which were done to that end.

6.   Whilest they were thus busied &
imployed, there came letters from the
Xogun that all the religious persons and
those that were banished for their religiō
should find ships at their owne charges,
to go out of the Country the October
following the which newes did increase
both the griefe, and the feruour of the
Christians, who were all distributed
into diuers Confraternities, thereby the
better and with greater vnion to helpe
one the other, as indeed by that meanes
they did exceedingly. But because it is
an easy matter through zeale & feruour
to grow to some, excesse therefore the
Fathers' tooke great care to counsayle
them they should behaue themselues in
such sort, that they did not exasperate
the Gentills, nor giue them occasion to
report, that the cause of the persecution
was some mutiny or rebellion on their
parts, and not only because they would
not deny the fayth of Christ: and particulerly

culerly they did procure that certaine
writings which they made amongſt
themſelues and ſubſcribed with their
names , what they would do in caſe that
the Fathers were put out of *Iapone* , and
themſelues forced to deny their ſayth ,
ſhould be done in that manner that the
Gentills ſhould haue no colour to calumniate them : the which was a matter of
very great importance & conſequence.

7. The feruour of the Chriſtians
increaſing dayly more & more , came at
legth to that paſſe that not cōtented with
their ſecret penances, they began (without euer conſulting the Fathers therein)
to make open proceſſions in the ſtreets ,
doing therein many publike penances .
About the beginning of May they made
one or two , all of them diſciplining
themſelues therein : and vpon the twelfe
day of the ſame moneth there went one
out of the Church of *All-Saintes* with
diuers kindes of penances in which there
were about a thouſand penitentes, ſome
carryng heauy croſſes on their backes ,

T 2   others

others being loaden with chaines of
Iron, others fiercely difciplining of the̅,
felues and the like, in this manner vifiting all the Churches of the towne, af-
king with weeping eyes mercy at God
Almighty his handes : and diuers children went in their company finging the
letanies with fuch deuotion, as moued
euen the hardeft harts to melt with forrow, and their eyes to fheed aboundant teares . In this manner they went
continuing their proceffion vntil there
were neyther ftreet nor Confraternity
in al the towne that did not make one or
two at the leaft .

8.   Within the Octaues of Pentecoft
there were made two very folemne pro-
ceffions; the firft was ordered by the Fathers of *S . Dominickes* Order , and therein were an exceeding number that did
difcipline themfelues , and diuers with
ropes tyed to their neckes and crownes
of pricking thornes vpon their heades .
The fecond was directed by the Fathers
of *S . Auguflines* Order , in which there
were

were ſome 500. perſons all clothed in
purple weedes carriyng heauy croſſes on
their backes, beſides diuers others that
went diſciplining of themſelues : ſo that
there was not ſcarce any one perſon in
all the Citty, man, womã, nor Child that
did not, ſome once, ſome twice, ſome
thrice go in theſe proceſſions, doing ſom
pennance or other therin, all with intention to moue Almighty God to mercy towardes them, and to ſhew the deſire they had by this meanes to prepare
themſelues to ſuffer ſome thing for the
loue of Chriſt. For concluſion of all, Father Prouinciall of the Society did ap-
point that a ſolemne proceſſion of the
bleſſed *Sacrament* ſhould be made in the
Colledge vpon *Corpus Chriſti* day, the
which was accordingly performed with
very great ſolemnity, cõcourſe of people
and deuotion, and after it the prayer of
40. houres was kept publikely, there being Sermons made both in the morning
and afternoone: wherin the people were
ſo moued to deuotion, to ſighes, and

T 3   teares

teares, that the Preacher at length could
scarce be heard for them : all which put
many in good hope that God would
heare their cryes and prayers, and eyther
tye the handes of those that were their
enemies, or giue them force and strength
to get the victory .

9 . This feruorous māner of proceeding , and to see moreouer that the Christians made so small account of temporall thinges , did cause such an amaze in
the seruantes of *Safioye*, who were Gentills , that they wrote forthwith vnto
their Lord (who was now comming
from the Court) signifiiyng vnto him
that the Citty was all in an' vprore , all
vnyted together and resolued not to obey
the *Xogun*, nor to let the Fathers depart
the country , paynting out the matter in
the worst manner that they could , and
aduising him he should be carefull and
consider how he came . If these letters
had come to *Safioye* his owne handes it
had beene an easy matter to haue infor-
med him of the truth and pacified all :
but

but the Meſſenger miſſing of him in the
way, went directly vnto the Court of
Surunga, and gaue them to a ſiſter of his
who was in great league with the *Xogun*,
and ſhe being a wicked woman, a Gentill and an enemy to the Chriſtian fayth,
went weeping with them vnto the *Xo-*
gun, and related the matter in ſuch manner, as though doubtleſſe her brethren
were both of them ſlaine already at
Nangaſaqui. Wherewithall the *Xogun*
was ſo moued to anger and indignation,
that laying his hand vpon his ſword, he
ſwore, that if *Nangaſaqui* were neere
hand he would go thither himſelfe in
perſon, and put it all to ſword and fire.
And fearing leaſt *Safioye* alone could
not be able to rule the Chriſtians and
bring them to due order and obedience,
he commanded that *Surungadono* one of
the principall Captaines which he had
in *Fuſhimi* ſhould go thither with all his
ſouldiers; and gathering together all the
reſt thereabout that were needful ſhould
execute that there which ſhould be

T 4 thought

thought most fitting and expedient.

How the Fathers of the Society of Iesus
were banished, & the Churches of
Nangasaqui *destroyed.*

CHAP. XV.

S A F I O Y D O N O at his arrinall at
Nangasaqui vpon the 23. of Iune,
hauing by the way done that in *A-*
rima which we mentioned in the 9.
Chapter, faw that all was quiet without
any mutiny or rebellion at all, and that
the feruour which the Chriftians had
fhewed was only to aske mercy at Gods
handes, and fhew that they were ready
to fuffer and giue their liues for Chrift.
Within two daies after his comming he
fent word vnto Father Prouinciall of
the Society, to the Superiours of the o-
ther Religious Orders, and vnto the Secular Prieftes, that they fhould all make
prouifion for fhipps in tyme, for that not
one of them, whether he were ftranger
or

or free-Denizen , should stay in the
Country , no not so much as any of the
youthes of the Seminary: the which caused a generall sorrow in all the Christians : although the newes which imediately came vpon it , that the ship of tra
ffique of the *Portugals* was safely arriued
from *China* thither , did not only ioy the
Gentills, but also gaue some comfort vnto them , for they hoped that vpon this
occasion the Gentills through the great
desire they haue to traffique with the *Por-*
tugalls , would wincke at them , at least
for a tyme : especially it being most certaine that the *Xogun* himselfe had shewed
great contentment when he heard thereof
of, and commanded that all fauour and
kind vsage should be shewed both to the
Captaine , and his Company .

2 . Hereupon *Father Prouinciall* delt
with the Captaine , and he very willingly offered himselfe to goe vnto the
Court to intreate of the *Xogun* , that at
the least he would permit one Church
in *Nangasaqui* , as the *Portugalls* & *Spani-*
ardes,

ardes , that liue there , and go and come
with their shipps , had euer had , and it
was thought the best course to intreat
Safioyedono to ioyne with the Captaine
in this petition to the *Xogun* , because o-
therwise infallibly it would be crossed
and neuer take effect . Whilest they were
busy in this consultations *Surungidono*
came with his souldiers from the Court
to *Nangasaqui* , and thinking to haue
found all the Country in Rebellion as it
was reported there , he found no signe at
all of any such thing , wherewithall he
shewed himselfe much disgusted , and
Safioyedono was no lesse with his comming thither. Whereupon they sent new
information vnto the Court , but neyther true nor fauourable towardes the
Christians , both because they knew the
Xogun could not endure thē & was resolued to destroy the Christianity of al his
Countries , and also because they would
not contradict one the other , nor rayse
any disgust or discontent among themselues, for of this and their owne interest
the

the Gentills of *Iapone* haue allwaies more regard , then eyther of reason , or iustice , equity , or Conscience .

3 . Both *Safioye* and *Surungadono* were vnwilling that the Captaine of the Portugal ship should go vnto the Court, saying that it would be an occasion of a greater breach if the *Xogun* should not graunt (as they thought he would not) that which the Captaine in perso should aske of him , and that it were far better to send an embassage vnto him with a present , the which although for this yeare perhapps it would not do much good , yet would it be a disposition for the yeare following, when his anger was once past,to get a grant of what they desired . There was no remedy but to follow their counsayle , because it was impossible that any thing could haue successe which was against their good liking : so thereupon foure or fiue Portugalls of good estimation were sent vnto the Court , and heareafter wee shall signify what effect their iourney had .

4 . In

4. In the meane while *Safioye* did not only follicite the departure of the Fathers by meanes of his own meffages, but alfo forced the Gouernours of the Citty, and the moft fubftantiall men of euery ftreet to enter into obligation, not to confent that any of the Fathers fhould remaine fecretly hidden, vnder paine of their liues, confifcation of their goods, and bondage of their wiues and children. The hope that the Fathers had that they might remaine at leaft fome of them in *Nangafaqui*, and from thence by little and little go recouering that which they had loft, did fomething mitigate the forrow which they conceyued for their Churches loft, and for the euill vfage of the Chriftians. But now feeing themfelues fruftrate of that hope, and that of force they muft forfake, & leaue defolate fo many foules which for fo long tyme they had guyded towards heauen, and inftructed in the knowledge and true feruice of Almighty God, with fo great labour, care, trauayle and paines, did
wound

wound their very heartes with griefe :
which was also much increased seeing
the teares, and hearing the lamentations
of those good Christians which continually came vnto them whilest they
remayned there, the which was now to
be but a very little while: for at that very
tyme there came from the Court the
finall resolution of all, which was, that
although the *Xogun* had receaued the
Embassage of the *Portugalls*, and promised them all fauour in such thinges as
concerned their trade and traffique, yet
as for other matters concerning the stay
of some of the Fathers in *Nangasaqui*,
there was no remedy ; saying that by
only granting or permitting them one
Church thereon other occasions hereto.
fore, they had by that meanes entred a-
gaine into all the Countries of *Iapone*,
and that therefore now he would see
if hee could put them out for good
and all.

5 . There were in all *Iapone* 22 .
Priestes, and fiue lay brethren of the holy
order

order of *S. Domnicke, S. Francis*, and *S. Austine*, seauen secular Priestes *Iaponians* borne, and foure or fiue of other inferiour Orders. Of the Society there were 117. Fathers and Brothers, besides that in their Seminary they had cōmonly 100. younge youthes, which they brought vp in learning and vertue to help towardes the conuersion of their Country; and almost as many more of good partes and sufficiency which did helpe to the same end were dispersed in diuers of the Fathers howses and Residences. The most of these by reasō of the necessity & want whereunto they were brought by the persecution, they were forced to dismisse, and some of those of the Seminary they left behind with persons of trust & confidence, because it was not possible to carry them all with them. All the Fathers did desire to remayne hid and disguised in *Iapone* to help the Christians and be partakers of their suffringes, but it could not be, by reason of the strict order that was taken against their stay,

and

and the extreme difficulty in fynding
meanes to keep them secret.

6 . The secular Priests and the other
religious persons consulted the matter
amongst themselues, and as many of
them remayned as could conueniently,
and Father Prouinciall of the Society
did send of his subiectes with all secrecy
into diuers places 18 . Fathers, and with
them nine brethren, and some Seminaristes, who with more security might
visit the Christians in the Fathers names
then they could themselues . Others of
the Fathers should haue retourned as
soone as the were out of the hauen, & so
remayned, but it could not possibly be
effectuated, by reason of the many spyes
and others that were set to watch of
purpose to hinder their designement
therein .

7 . For all those persons that were
to go into banishment, there were but
three shippes, and those little ones, and
very ill prouided . Vpon Saturday being
the 25 . of October, *Safioye* sent word,
                                    cōmanding

comanding them that vpon the 27. in any cafe they fhould imbarke themfelues, and if thofe fhipps were not ready then, they fhould all go vnto *Fucunda* which is another port towne thereby. They had already taken all the pictures out of the Churches : and after they had comunicated al that were defirous to receiue the B. Sacrament & confummated that which did remayne thereof, they made their laft Sermons vnto the Chriftians whome they were to leaue behind them there, how they fhould behaue themfelues in the confeffió of their faith encouraging them to conftancy, with affurance that by the grace of God that tempeft would quietly ceafe and could not long endure. The bodies of diuers holy Martyrs that had beene buried in their Churches, they tooke vp & fecretly layd them in diuers places where they might remayne fecure, and be kept with reuerent refpect vntill fome better tyme. The fame they did with the bodies of diuers of the Fathers and brethren there
buried

buried who had with great cure & zeale
laboured in the cultiuating that parcell
of Chriftes vineyard , becaufe they
fhould not be abufed and profaned by
the Gentills, enemies of Chrifts true religion . Finallie thefe thinges being al con-
cluded , vpon the 27 . of October in the
yeare 1614, the Gentills tooke poffeffion
of all their Churches. The greater part
of the religious men , and the reft that
were appointed to banifhement , were
carried to *Fucunda*, and there put in little
Cottages of fifhermen, and kept by Officers that watched them both by fea and
lande . Others , togeather with Father
Prouinciall remayned in a place neere
Nangafaqui fiue or fixe daies vntill fuch
tyme as the fhipps were all prepared .

8 . And in this place dyed Father
Iames Mefquita a man of great vertue
wifdome and induftry in the conuerfion
of the Gentills of that country of *Iapone*
where he had liued well nigh fourty
yeares . He came from thence into *Europe*
diuers yeares ago for tutor and condu-

V   ctor

ctor of those tower Gentlemé that came
in the name of the Christian Princes of
Bungo, *Arima*, and *Omura* to kisse Pope
Gregorie the 13. his feet, and King *Philip*
the second his hands, and after that so
long iorney he spent many yeares in the
conuersion and instruction of the people
of those countries of whome he was exceedingly beloued. His sicknes was occasioned as was thought by the griefe he
tooke to see the present iniuries & cala-
mities of those poore afflicted Christians. Meanes was made to *Saficye* that he
might be carried into the Citty to be cured there, but he would not permit it by
any meanes, and so being carried to a
little straw cabbin of a poore Fisherman
there he dyed with wounderous ioy and
comfort of his soule vpon the first day
of Nouember, hauing suffered in his life
tyme very much for the propagation of
the fayth, and glory of our blessed Sauiour.

9. The Gentills soone after they had
taken the Christians Churches into
their

their handes with great contempt began
to pull them downe and burne the wood
therof, as they had done in *Meaco* and
Ozaca : but this ioy did not endure long,
for that not long after there came newes
that the Kingdome was all in an vprore
by reaſon of a falling out betwixt the old
Xogun & *Fideyori* the ſonne of *Taycoſama*,
who was laſt Emperour, as ſhallbe ſhewed at the end of the ſecond part of this
Relation.

10. Vpon the 7. & 8. of Nouember did
ſet to ſayle the glorious fleet of Religious
perſons, & *Iaponian* Gentlemen ſent in baniſhment for the fayth of Chriſt, & they
went in this maner. In one ſhip that went
vnto the Philipine Ilandes there were the
Fathers of *S. Dominicke*, *S. Frauncis*, & *S.
Auguſtines* Orders, 8. Fathers of the Society, 15. Brethren, and 15. Seminariſtes,
and with them *Don Iuſto*, and *Don Iohn*
with their Families, and other Gentlemen baniſhed from *Meaco*. In the other
two which went for *Macan* a Port town
of *China* there went more then threeſcor

Fathers and Brethren of the Society, and more then fifty *Seminariftes*. And this was the fucceffe of the perfecution and banifhment of the Fathers, vntill the 8. of Nouember 1614. That which happened afterwardes fhalbe related in the fecond Part: although it feemeth conuenient firft in one or two Chapters more to ad to this a breife narration of the Heroicall actes and vertues of *Don Iufto*, and of his arriuall at the *Philippines*.

Of the arriuall of the Fathers of the Society at Macan *, and* Manilla *; and of the notable vertues of* Don Iufto.

CHAP. XVI.

IT is not hard to coniecture in what affliction the poore Chriftians of *Iapone* remayned, feeing thefelues now without Prieftes and Paftours, their Churches caft downe and burned, and all the Country fwarming with Souldiers

diers, not knowing what would be the end & euent of so tempestuous a storme, yet much more was the griefe of the Fathers, who were by violence separated from their spirituall Children, whome by the Ghospell of Christ Iesus they had begotten vnto God, & whome therefore they most entirely loued, & whose good they most earnestly desired. This only comforted them, that they hoped to returne vnto them shortly disguised, if they could not otherwise; and also to see them with such courage to suffer for their fayth when they departed from them.

2. The two ships that went for *Macan* ariued safely there within few dayes, as both the way being shorter, and the ships much better then that which went vnto the *Philipines*, which being but an old vessell not well prouided, and so loaden with passengers that they could scarce stand one by another, was therefore much feared would miscary by the way. And this feare was much augmen-

men-

mented by meanes of two shipps of *Hollanders* which being in *Firando* meant to haue set out after them and taken them, the which infallibly they would haue done, had not the Lord of that Citty, though a Gentil, hindred them. The Fathers of the Society did not thinke to haue sent more then eight or ten vnto the Philippines, and scarce had they taken roome for so many in the ship, and therfore when afterwardes it fell out to be precisely necessary that eight and thirty should go therein, they were so straightned and pestered, that therewithall & by reason of other incommodities there dyed two of the Fathers, and two of the brethren: two of them whilest they were at sea, and the other two imediatly after their comming to land.

3. *F. Antony Francis de Critana* was the first of them that dyed at sea, a man of threescore and eight yeares old whereof he had spent thirty in *Iapone* with great example of sanctity, holines of life and zeale of soules. He was Minister

ſter of the Colledge of *Nangaſaqui*, and
tooke ſuch paines at the tyme of their departure thence, that with very wearines,
and the foreſaid ſtriatnes, without any
other infirmity, he dyed: and becauſe he
was of notorious vertue, and dyed in baniſhment for the fayth of Chriſt, he
was reuerenced of all the religious men
that went in the ſhip, as a worthy Con-
feſſor of Chriſt. He dyed within ſight of
land, and therefore the Captaine of the
ſhip with diuers of the religious perſons
carried his body vnto an Hermitage by
the ſhore ſide, from whence afterward it
was conueyed to the Citty & Colledge
of *Manilla*, where within a few dayes they
arriued after a mouethes nauigation,
wherein they had had much ſoule weather and diuers cruell ſtormes.

4. Before I relate the maner of inter-
taynment which was made in *Manilla* to
Don Iuſto, *Don Iohn* and their Company,
it will not be amiſſe to ſhew briefly
who they where, and ſet downe ſome
part of that which they did and ſuffered

for

for the fayth of Chrift , and for his holy
Church. This *Don Iufto* was borne in
the Kingdome of *Tzunocuni* , not far off
from the Citty of *Meaco:* his Fathers
name was *Darius Findadono* , his Mothers *Mary:* he was of the noble and
auncient houfe and linage of *Tacayama*
which doth fignify a High mountayne ,
and it agreed well vnto them , for both
the Father and the Sonne were men of
great vertue , excellent example , and
finguler defenders of all the Chriftianity of *Cami* , a great part of the Country
fo called . *Findadono Don Iufto* his Father
was alwaies held and efteemed for a
very worthy Captaine and exceeding
wife , much giuen whileft he was a Gentil to the ftudy of the *Iaponian* Sectes and
fuperftitious worfhip of their Idolles ,
from which he was brought by this
meanes .

5 .   Father *Gaspar Vilela* , and one
Laurence a Brother of the Society had
preached the Chriftian fayth in *Meaco* ,
for the fpace of fiue or fix yeares , with
                                        fuch

such opposition of the *Bonzi* and Gentills , that the fruit of their labours was but very small : many tymes they went about to haue killed them , or banished them, holding and reputing them as barbarous & ignorant persons , as enemies of the *Caynies* & *Fotoques*, & of the peace and quiet of the Kingdome . At the petition of the Bonzi , the examination of their cause was committed vnto two Gentlemen very earnest in the superstitions of the Gentills , who one day meaning to make a mockery of a certaine Christian , aked him certaine questions about the Christian fayth. He at the first modestly excused himselfe alleadging his ignorance , as being no scholler , and a simple man , but afterwardes he answered the best he could . They vrged him with difficultyes more and more , and he so well behaued himselfe in answering, that their iesting and mockery turned to good earnest in the end: for that they seeing themselues conuinced with the reasons which he did alledge, desired him in

V 5   and

any cafe he would bring them a preacher becaufe they meant purpofely to heare al that could be faid . It was feared that this was only a trappe layd the better thereby to take the Father, yet did he fend Brother *Laurence* aforfaid vnto thē, who through the help & grace of God , did fo worke with thē that when the Father himfelfe came vnto them as he did foone after, he found wolues turned into lambes, and the men wholy changed from that they were before, fo that after they were inftructed fufficiently he did baptize them , and diuers other who were moued by their example, and by that meanes the ftorme for that tyme did ceafe, to the great griefe and difcredit of the Bonzi.

6 . There was great fpeach in the Court of the ftrange mutation of thefe two Gentlemen, and *Findadono* among the reft did vfe to ieft at them very much, it feeming to him an eafy thing to con-uince the Brother in fauour of their Sectes . Inquiring therefore where he was,

was, he went vnto him , heard his Sermons, argued, questioned, disputed with
him diuers tymes, but such was the light
and euidence of the truth of the Catholique religion, that he found himselfe
(though meruailing at himselfe) wholly
conuinced therewith , and so was not
only himselfe baptized, but carrying the
Father to his Castle of *Sana*, he caused
him also to instruct and baptize his wife,
Children , and kinred , and some 100 .
Gentlemen of his house . He desired his
owne name should be *Darius*, his wifes
Mary , and his eldest sonne *Iustus* who
was then 15 . yeares old ; this happened
the yeare 1565 . in which yeare also was
conuerted and baptized *Don Iohn Naytodono* of fourteene yeares of age , Lord
of almost all the Kingdome of *Tamba* ,
a young Gentlemen of great expectation.
By *Darius* his meanes and example , he
was moued to be a Christian , and was
companion then vnto *Don Iustus* in
baptisme, as he was now in banishment .

7 . This

7. This therefore may be the first
comendation of these two noble souldiers of Christ to haue perseuered so
firme and constant so many yeares in the
fayth they once receaued, against all the
power of the deuill, neyther being moued with the comand of three most potent Emperours *Nobnnanga*, *Taycosama*
and the *Xogun* that now reigneth, nor
mollified with the continuall perswasions and example of the Princes, Lords
and noble Men of *Iapone*, nor terrified
with persecutions, losses of their estates
liuinges, goods, and honor, nor with
the continuall dangers of their liues to
do any thinge in preiudice of the profession of their faith, nor (which is yet
more) carried away with the stronge
streame of licentious life, which in that
country is of mighty force, all liberty in
that kind being granted to men of their
yeares and quality to do any thinge indecent or ill beseeming Christian Gentlemen; and all this hauing no example
at all, nor any other thinge besides their
fayth

fayth and religion that might oblige or
moue the thereunto, but only the fpeaches
fermons, and perfwafions of a few poore
religious men, that were meere ftrangers vnto them, of no authority, command, or power in the Country, but rather much hated, difgraced, and abafed
by the *Bonzi*, and moft of thofe that did
profeffe the Religion of *Iapone*.

8. Their fecond comendation may
be, for the great zeale they alwayes
fhewed in defending of the Church, &
minifters thereof in the great combates
and contradictions which it had in the
beginning thereof. Immediatly almoft
after they were baptized *Miyoridono*, and
Daniedono Don Iohns vnckle, killed the
Cubofama, who was then the Lord of all
Iapone, the *Bonzi* who were then great
with the *Dayri* (who was the true owner
of the Empire) tooke that opportunity
to get the Fathers banifhed by publique
proclamation from the *Dayri*, confifca-
ting their Houfe and Church, and very
hardly letting them paffe with life. In
this

this occasion these worthy Gentlemen were the principall defence, and almost only refuge the Fathers had in almost three yeares that their banishment endured. And when *Nobunanga* entred *Meaco* by force of armies, *Darius* and *Don Iusto* by *Vatadono* his meanes who was Gouernour of *Meaco*, got the restored in honorable sorte, with ample Patentes from the new *Cubosama*, and *Nobunanga* to preach the Ghospell freely where they pleased, in despite of all the *Bonzi* and of the *Oayri* himselfe. And all the tyme that Nobunanga liued, who fauoured *Don Iusto* very much, they were perpetuall defenders and vpholders of the Fathers in many great and grieuous persecutions, raysed against them by the *Bonzi*, exposing many tymes to danger for their sakes their estates, their honors and their liues.

9.   Exceeding great likewise was the zeale they had of the conuersion of soules vnto the Christian fayth. In the tyme *Don Iohn* was Lord of the Kingdome

dome of *Tamba* (for afterwardes he loſt
it in the tyme of *Nobunanga* his warrs)
he was the cauſe of great good therein
in that kind . The Country of *Tucacuqui*
whereof *Darius* & *Don Iuſto* were Lords
was full of *Bonzi* , hauing many ancient
Temples therein, and very much inhabited by a ſort of Gentills that were moſt
obſtinate : yet ſuch was their zeale , their
care and induſtry , that partly by entreaties , partly by benefittes , partly by diſ-
putations they moued and perſwaded
many to imbrace the Chriſtian fayth ;
ſo that within few yeares there remayned not ſo much as one Gentill in all the
Coûtry, nor any Temple that eyther was
not deſtroied , or turned into a Church ,
nor a *Bonzo* that was not eyther conuerted , or els went willingly away vnto
ſome other place. The like they did in
another Country that was giuen by *Nobunanga* : and in *Acaxi* they begon to do
the ſame . By which may well be gathered the exceeding great number of Gentills , that by their induſtry and meanes
receaued

receaued the Chriſtian faith . They builded many Churches in all the townes ,
ſet vp many croſſes in high wayes and
vpon montaines , helping in all thinges
the Fathers of the Society that had care
there of the conuerſion and inſtruction
of the people ; and being ſtill the firſt in
prayer , pennance , and all other pious
workes as Fathers and Mayſters of their
ſubiectes , to the great admiration of all
the Gentills that liued theraboutes.

10 .   The ſame pious offices did they
likewiſe exerciſe being at the Court a-
mong other Lords and Noble men . For
Don Iuſto in particuler being ſo wiſe
and prudent , and ſo eſteemed as he was
generally of them all , would neuer let
occaſion paſſe , but by one meanes or
other he would procure to giue notice
to them all , of the truth and ſolidity of
Chriſtian beliefe , and of the falſhood &
errors of their ſectes , and that with ſuch
efficacity , that all the moſt principall
Chriſtians of the Court were conuerted
by his perſwaſion or example , and the
Gentills

Gentills that were the Fathers friends
were al gained by his meanes. Info much
that for diuers yeares the Gentills called
the Christian religion the religion of *Tacayama*, not knowing other name for it
but this of *Don Iusto*, who was so zealous
a professor therof.

11. Their integrity and examplar
life was also very notable. *Darius* being
now old, gaue ouer his estate and gouerment to spend his tyme in the chiefe busines of the saluation of his soule and the
conuersion of his subiectes to the fayth
of Christ, and so dyed a very holy and a
happy death in the yeare 1595. And *Don
Iusto* his integrity and purity of life was
so great, he being a most noble and couragious gentleman, in the very flower of
his age, and in the middest of manifold
euill occasions, that *Taycosama* the Emperour himselfe did highly comend him
for the same, not without great wonde-
ing thereat. And many noble men that
were conuinced in their vnderstanding
of the truth and verity of Christian reli-
X gion

gion by the sermons which they heard
sayd, that the reasons why they were
not baptized, was because they could not
liue a continent life, in that manner as
Don Iusto did, it being a thing vnworthy
to a noble man, or to an honest mind to
professe a religion, and not liue accordingly therto.

12.   They were all also most deuout
vnto the holy Sacramentes, continually
frequenting the same, and all other actions of religious piety: and so great was
the respect they bare vnto the Fathers,
who were their spirituall guydes and
Maysters, that it was noted in *Don Iusto*,
that in the space of fifty yeares in which
he dayly conuersed with them, he was
neuer heard, nor knowne to speake so
much as one only vnreuerent word to
any one of them all, for whatsoeuer
cause or occasion that was offered. And
which is more, notwithstanding all the
good he did vnto them, and for the
Church and generall cause of all the
Christians, or euills that he suffered for
the

the ſame ; it ſeemed vnto him to haue
beene very ſmall , and not more but that
which he was bound to do in honour :
and yet three ſeuerall tymes had he for
them , and for his fayth and religion left
his liuing and eſtate , loſt his honor and
reputation , and his life alſo , as far as lay
in him to doe.

13. The firſt tyme was ſoone after
he was a Chriſtian vpon this occaſion.
Araqui the Lord of the Kingdome of
Tzunocuni a great friend and benefactor
of his , did determine to ryſe againſt *No-*
bunanga and ioyne with his enemies.
Don Iuſto was afflicted therewithall , and
did all his endeauour poſſible to make
them friendes : and to oblige *Araqui* the
more vnto him , he did renew an oath of
fidelity and freindſhip which before he
had made vnto him , and gaue vnto him,
as hoſtages and pledges of his fayth his
only Sonne , and a ſiſter of his owne,
who was then but a child . Hereupon
Araqui put the matter into his handes,
and being in his iourney towards the

Court

Court about that busines, an enemy of
Don Iusto perswaded *Araqui* that he was
betrayed : and that if he went he would
loose both his estate and life . It was a
false report, yet *Araqui* giuing credit
thereunto, retyred backe, and declared
himselfe for an enemy to *Nobunanga*, &
Don Iusto for many reasons could not
choose but follow him, and take his
part .

14 . *Nobunanga* had notice thereof,
raysed a great power, and came against
them, vsing first many meanes to draw
Don Iusto to his part, because he knew
him to be a very great Captaine, that he
had a troup of gallant men, and a For-
tresse that was almost inuincible : but
seeing it was not possible, he tooke for
the last meanes this, which was to send
him word, that seeing the Christian religion doth teach right and iustice to be
done, that he should leaue the freindship
of *Araqui*, who without cause and a-
gainst all right, reason, iustice and equity had made himselfe an enemy vnto
him :

him : and that if he did not , he would
deſtroy the Churches and Chriſtians in
his Kingdomes , and crucify the Fathers
euen before his eyes : that he ſhould therefore conſider well what he meant to
do .

15. This meſſage was more terrible
to *Don Iuſto* then death it ſelfe would
haue beene : for on the one ſyde the
friendſhip and great obligations he had
to *Araqui* , the oath he had made vnto
him , the pledges which he had giuen
him , his only Sonne and Siſter , who
were innocentes, & ſhould be doubtleſſe
ſlaine if he yealded vnto *Nobunanga* , the
ſpeach of the world that he was not loy-
all to his friend ; and aboue all that his
Father *Darius* and his Captaines , whereof the greater part were Gentills , in no
caſe would conſent thereto : theſe reaſons I ſay did moue him very much not
to leaue , but ſtill to ſtand to *Araqui* .
And on the other ſide the deſtruction of
the Chriſtians and Churches , and the
death of the Fathers who were already
X 3 priſoners

prisoners in *Nobunangas* Campe, did
greatly vrge the contrary. He consulted
with one of the Fathers whome *Nobunanga* sent vnto him, and by him he vnderstood that the oath which he had
made to *Araqui*, did not bynd him, by
reason it was only made with intention
to make him and *Nobunanga* friendes:
but yet the reasons afore mentioned, togeather with the teares of his mother,
and his wife, would not permit him yet
to make any resolution: and so the Father returned to the campe to dye with
the rest of his companions, *Darius* and
his Captaines all this while knowing
nothing of the businesse. *Don Iusto* then
replenished with griefe, full of doubt
and perplexity which way to turne him
selfe, entred into his Oratory, and there
casting himselfe downe before a Cruci-
fix, he did at length resolue himselfe, not
without aboundant teares, to sacrifice
to God, as another *Abraham*, his only
Sonne, his sister, his honor, and estate,
and all he had. Which being done he
wrote

wrote a briefe letter , and very secretly
only with two pages attending on him ,
went forthwith after the Father , and
kneeling downe vpon his knees , he cut
of his owne haire in signe of leauing off
the world : his two pages he sent backe
vnto his Father and his Captaines with
the letter he had written , wherein he
said , that seeing himselfe in that occasiõ
in wonderous perplexity he found no o-
ther remedy but only death , and seeing
that it was not lawfull to kill himselfe (as
the *Iaponians* often do in such occasions)
he had determined to dye vnto the
world : that they should defend the For-
tresse and the Country from *Araqui* ,
and he would go to dye , or be banished
with the Fathers , whose disciple now he
had made himselfe , by dying to the
world .

16 . *Darius* , and the rest remayned
astonished with this newes : and fearing
least they might come by other meanes
to *Araqui* his eares , and thereupon his
Daughter and Grandchild be put to
X 4   some

some cruel and vntimely death, he tooke
post presently, and went to *Araqui* himselfe, protesting that he did not know of
his Sonnes resolution, and that he came
to dye insteed of those two innocentes
which he had as hostages. Diuers there
were that counsailed *Araqui* to crucify
both him and the two Children for an
example to all others: but he did not
consent thereto, wondering much both
at *Iusto* and *Darius* act, and only caused
them to be put in prison for a tyme. *Nobunanga* and all with him did highly
commend *Don Iusto* his deed, and sending for him to come vnto his Pallace,
he answered that he came not thither to
serue him but to dy or be banished with
the Fathers: but God Almighty who
meant only to proue and try him, did so
dispose, that *Araqui* was ouercome, his
wife, children, kinsfolkes, & freindes
all killed and crucified. *Darius* and the
two Children set free and safe deliuered,
and that he was both more honored then
before, and his estate increased, and the

Fathers

Fathers and Christians by his meanes, more fauoured. And this was the first occasion in which he shewed his loue to his Religion, to the Fathers, and the cómon Cause.

17. The second was in the tyme of *Quambacu* or *Taycofama.* A certaine Captaine called *Aquechi* killed *Nobunanga* in the yeare 1582. and *Don Iusto* was one of the priucipall that did reuenge his death and brake the army of the enimies, and thereby was a great occasion that *Quambacu* did succeed in the Empire, for which cause he was very much esteemed of him, and the Christians greatly fauoured in that manner, and that he was not held for a man of discretion that had not heard the Sermons of the Catechisme at *Don Iustos* perswasion. By which meanes many noble personages were made Christians and baptized. This prosperity did endure vntill the yeare 1587. in which *Quambacu* did set vpon the conquest of the Kingdomes of *Ximo*, in which warres his principall Captaines

were

were all Chriftians , *Don Iufto* , *Don Au-*
guftine , *Condera* , *Simeon* , the Lordes of
Bungo , *Arima* , and *Omura* , and others :
fo great feruour being in the Campe that
all was hearing of Sermons, and making
Croffes in their banners : but all this
was turned vpfide downe, by the ac-
cufation of an old *Bonzo* called *Yacuin*
vpon this occafion.

18.   *Quambacu* had giuen vnto *Don*
Iufto the eftate of *Acaxi* , and the *Bonzi*
therof thinking doubtleffe they fhould
be thereby vtterly vndone, before he
came to take poffeffion, they all of them
went with their Idolls vnto *Quambacu*
his mother, to aske mercy and fauour by
meanes of this *Yacuin* , who was very
great with her, alledging that *Don Iufto*
was a deftroyer of Idols and Temples ,
and therefore they intreated fhe would
be a meanes that they , their Temples
with their reuenewes might be freed &
fauoured , But *Don Iufto* held himfelfe
for much abufed by them, that they
would accufe him in the Court, he hauing

uing done no iniury at all vnto them, for
which cause he would giue no eare vnto
them . They departed with many Complaintes against him , and *Tacuin* rested
very desirous to reuenge himselfe of this
which he esteemed a disgrace, & of the
destruction of his Idolls .

19 .   Comming therefore from the
Country of *Arima*, he complayned vnto
Quambacu, that the Fathers had perswaded *Arimadono* to take from him certaine
Christiã Gentlewomen which he meant
to haue brought to him for bad intents
and purposes . He extolled very much
their beauty , comelines of person , and
the like, protesting that the Fathers were
much more obeyed in that Country then
his Highnes , and that it was intolerable
that a strange religion should be permitted to florish so much within the Kingdome of *Iapone* , and that *Don Iusto* went
vp and downe folliciting all the could ,
that the Temples and Idolls might be vtterly destroied , the *Bonzi* banished , and
the people made Christians by maine
force,

force, alledging also what he had seene
and knowne done in *Tacazuqui*, *Acaxi*
Bunga, *Arima*, & other partes. *Quambacu*
with this complaint was much moued
vnto wrath, & comanded the Fathers to
be banished, the Churches ouerthrown
and that all the Lordes should eyther
leaue their Fayth, or loose their landes,
liuinges, and estates.

20.   The principall Combat was
now against *Don Iusto*, to whome some
friends of his carried the message, and
vsed many perswasions vnto him to accomodate himselfe vnto the tyme. He
answered constantly that he was ready
to giue his life and liuing for *Quambacu*,
but much more for the fayth of Christ,
and that therefore if they loued him,
they should not so much as mention any
such matter any more. There was none
there that durst carry this answere backe
to *Quambacu* : whereupon he rising vp
said : I will my selfe tell him so much
vnto his face, and I will carry my sword
also with me, that his Maiesty may with

it

it cut off my head for this cauſe if he
pleaſe. Whereupon *Quambacu* commanded
that he ſhould be baniſhed, and he accepted it with outward ſignes of great
internall ioy. This only was a griefe
vnto him, to ſee ſo many gallant men
as he had attending on him, al vnproui-
ded and reduced to pouerty vpon this
occaſion: for it is the cuſtome in *Iapone*,
that the Lord or maiſter being baniſhed,
all that hould liuinges or landes of him
do imediatly looſe them all. But neyther
this nor the teares of his friends, nor the
perſwaſions of many Princes and Lords
could moue him any thing at all. So did
he now depart from the Court alone &
with diſgrace, where a little before he
had entred with great honor and triumph, and liued in great eſteeme and
reputation. His parentes, wife, children
and kinred left vpon this newes the For-
treſſe and Eſtate of *Acaxi*, and did retire
themſelues vnto a poore village of the
mountaine Country, where his Father
Darius made an holy end of this miſera-
ble

ble and mortall life, and he himfelfe went
fecretly to feeke the Fathers of the Society, who becaufe they would not leaue
the Country and Chriftians defolate,
lay hidden priuately in the Iland of *A-
macafa*, where when he came he made
the fpirituall Exercife with very great
deuotion, and therein a Generall Confeffion of all his life fince his firft being
a Chriftian, ioyfull to fee himfelfe now
freed from the world, and greatly defirous to begin a new religious life. And
Almighty God did fo ordaine, that the
Lordes and Nobles of the Court did
euen ftriue among themfelues to receiue
& giue intertainement to the Captaines
and Gentlemen that had beene his followers, who afterward were occafion
of exceeding great good, and of the
fpreading of the Chriftiã fayth in many
Kingdomes.

21.   More then a yeare did *Don Iufto*
liue in pouerty and obfcurity, & *Quambacu* then feeing that he could not ouercome his conftancy, nor with honor
                                    reftore

restore him to his former place and dignity , he commanded the Lord of the
Kingdomes of *Canga*, *Noto*, and *Yetchu*,
who had been *Don Iusto* his equall a smal
tyme before, that he should keepe him
in his Country, and giue him necessary
allowance for his maintenance . Six and
twenty yeares he liued in those Kingdomes with an inuincible courage and
constancy of mind , and rare exemplar
life , alwaies prepared to giue his life for
Christ . And that which deserueth admiration is , that being so stout of mind
and full of mettall as he was , and seeing
that other persons that were nothing in
respect of him did rise to great estates &
dignities , and that only because he was
a Christian did liue in perpetual disgrace
and continuall danger also ; yet did he
neuer giue so much as once a signe of
any sadnes , nor euer made complaint
thereof, but being euer merry, laughed at
the world : although *Figendono* gaue him
fiue and twenty thousand *Gocus* of rent
euery yeare, which do equall almost our
Ducates

Ducates of *Europe*, wherewith he liued in good and honorable fashion. After *Quambacu* his death, he buylded three or foure Churches in thofe Kingdomes, hauing alwaies with him fome of the Fathers of the Society, with *Figendono* his leaue, who was the Lord of thofe Countries, whofe loue and affection he had gayned in fuch fort, that publikely he would not fticke to fay, that there was no meanes to obtaine faluation but in the Chriftian Religion, the which in fhort tyme increafed fo much in thofe Kingdomes, that it feemed to florifh there the moft of any place in all *Iapone*, many of the inhabitantes being newly conuerted and baptized, and very many that were banifhed from other places, for their fayth, being called thither by *Don Iufto* his meanes, and honorably prouided for and maynteyned there by *Figendonoes* order and appointment.

22. And one of thefe was *Don Iohn Navtodono*, together with his fonne *Don Thomas*, for that after he had loft the Kingdome

Kingdóe of *Tamba*, & wandred through
many Kingdomes, he was at length in-
tertayned and much esteemed by *Don*
Augustine ; who gaue vnto them both
very great rentes and reuenewes in his
country , and they with their great zeale
and exemplar life did much helpe and
further the Christians thereof , vntill at
length in the yeare 1601 . *Canzuyedono*
Lord of *Fingo*, after *Don Augustines*
death and ouerthrow , did rayse a cruell
persecution againſt the Church, in which
they both of them suffered exceeding
much. For after many intreaties and perſwaſions to make them leaue their fayth,
he confiſcated their landes , houſes and
liuinges, commanding them vpon paine
of their liues not to go out of the Country , and that no body ſhould receaue
them into their houſes, nor ſell them any
meate ; nor buy any thing for them : taking away alſo their Children from
them, comanding and threating to keep
them vntill they paid a great ſume of money, ſo that they were compelled to make
    Y   themſelues

themselues little houses or Cabbines of
ftraw, wherein they and their wiues
& family liued for the space of six
monthes: at the end whereof feeing
their conftancy, he tooke from them all
he pleafed, and then expelled them out
of the Country almoft naked. In this
tyme they both of them wrote moft feruorous letters, worthy to be read, vnto
the reft of the Chriftians, animating
them to conftancy and perfeuerance,
manifefting therein alfo their owne defires, to dye for Chrift. *Don Iufto* hauing intelligence of their miferies, and
afflictions, delt with *Figendono* who knew
them very well, to fend for them, and
giue them entertainement: Almighty
God fo difpofing it, to the end that as
they had beene companions in their
fayth, in baptifme, zeale and examplar
life, fo they fhould alfo be in banifhment,
which is a kind of prolonged martyrdome.

Of

Of their receauing at Manilla *, and of the death of* Don Iusto .

CHAP. XVII.

THIS was their estate when the third and last tempest was raysed against them (as I mentioned in the VIII . Chapter , wherein they were by the *Xoguns* order sent to *Nangasaqui* : there they liued with meruailous example vntill the end of October , spending their tyme in pyous actions and workes of Charity . *Don Thomas* and others made the spirituall exercise there (*Don Iohn* could not by reason of his sicknesse) with such deuotion as they seemed rather religious persons , then such as they were . After *Don Iusto* his death there was found a paper written with his hand of the good motions , heauenly comfortes & consolations which God had bestowed vpon him at diuers times. At his being in *Nangasaqui* diuers
Gentill

Gentill Lordes did send to visit him ,
desiring to deale with the *Xogun* to send
for him to the Court: and *Fideyori Tay-*
cosamaes Sonne desired much to haue him
for his Captaine Generall of *Ozaca* : but
he made small account of all these offers,
saying he would not change his banishment for all the world . It is certaine that
before he tooke shipping he kwew he
should dy very soone, so that in the 150.
dayes which passed betwixt the sentence
of his banishment , and the tyme of his
taking shippe, he alwaies was expecting
death , and that with such quietnes and
ioy , as if he had beene then in his chiefe
prosperity : in so much that *Yetchuydono*
Lord of the Kingdome of *Bugen* his
great freind, hauing vnderstood thereof,
although he were a Gentil sayd: *Yea mar-*
ry Sir , with this Don Iusto doth seale vp
the rest of his worthy deedes and excellent
exploites; and if he had not done so, he should
haue disgraced himselfe and obscured them .

2 .   Their Iorney by sea was not a
little troublesome vnto them, they neuer

uer hauing beene acquainted with Sea
voyages before, and carrying with them
besydes so many women and Children.
But letting this passe : as soone as in *Manilla* notice was giuen of their arriuall,
there was a generall ioy in all desiring to
giue them all intertainement possible,
and in particuler the Gouernour thereof
Don Iohn de Silua, who had heard much
of *Don Iusto*, sent a Galley well appointed
and therein some persons of account to
giue him the welcome, and to offer him
all courtesy. The wynd being contrary it
was three or foure daies ere they could
come to land. When they landed all the
great Artillery was shot off to welcome
them, and all the whole Citty, and the
religious persons thereof went vnto the
Sea shoare the meet and receiue them, as
holy Confessors of Christ, accompanying
them vnto the Pallace, where the Gouernour and Iudges did imbrace them
with all kindnes, congratulating their
comming thither, and the courage they
had shewed in suffering so much for
Y 3

their

their fayth as they had done, offering
vnto them both in their owne behalfes
and in the kinges, whatsoeuer should be
necessary or conuenient for them. *Don
Iusto* in most courteous manner gaue
them thankes for the great fauour and
honor they had done to them, they being
altogether vnworthy thereof, as not hauing beene so happy to giue their liues
for Christ: and so taking their leaues of
them, they were accompanied by the
Cittizens vnto the Colledg of the Society of Iesus, passing in the way by the
great Church, and by the Monastery of
S. Augustine at the intreaty of the Clergy,
and Religious persons, who came out of
their gats to receiue them with musicke
and solemnity. The like was done the
day following, by the Fathers of the orders of *S. Dominicke*, and *S. Francis*, all
kind of persons desiring to shew their
forwardnes in honoring and entertay-
ning them.

3. *Don Iusto* liued only fourty dayes
after his arriuall at *Manilla*, and in that
                                     tyme

tyme he was often visited by the Gouernour, by the Archbishop, by the Religious men, and all the principall persons
of the Citty, all of them conceiuing a
great loue and affection towardes him,
and making no lesse esteeme of him then
his worthinesse deserued. But he taking
small delight in any thing of this world,
desired nothing so much as a house a
part, where freed from visitation and
complementes, he might without distra-
ction attend to the chiefe busines of his
soule, saying he feared very much least
God would pay him in this life, for that
small seruice some did imagine he had
done him. It seemeth that Almighty God
did meane to proue this his worthy
souldier as he did his seruant *Iob*, and
that he would honor him both in life &
death in signe of the great crowne he
would giue him in heauen, for his great
courage and constancy in his fayth. For
that eyther through the chang of ayre &
clymates or differences of meates, or
through the incomodities he had endured

red in his banishment and navigation (very contrary both to his nature, yeares, and complexion) he fell sicke of a continuall feuer, accompanied with a bloudy flux, the which in small tyme brought him to his end.

4. He knew presently that this disease was mortall, and so he began to prepare himselfe for death, and sayd vnto his Confessour : *Father, I perceaue that I growe towardes my end, although I make no shew of it, because of not discomforting my family. I am very well content, and comforted therewithall, it being Gods holy will and pleasure, especially among so many religious persons, and in so Christian a countly as this is. I pray you render many thanks in my behalfe vnto the Lord Gouernour, the Archbishop, Iudges, Religious men, and all the rest, for the courtesy, fauour, and honor they haue done me. As for my Wife, Daughter & Grandchildren take no care, for I take none at all : they and I am banished for Christes cause. I do much esteeme the loue they haue alwaies borne me, and that they would accompany*

pany

*pany me hither ; I hope that Almighty God
for whose sake they are now in a strang country, will be a true Father vnto them, and so
they shall haue no want of me.* He made
a *Testament*, such another as holy *Tobias*
did, comending vnto them perseuerance
in their fayth, and obedience vnto the
Fathers, and that if any of them did not
well, the rest should aduise and counsaile them, and tell the Fathers of them :
and if they did not obey, they should be
depriued of their inheritance, and of the
name of his house & Family. This done
he receaued the holy Sacramentes with
great deuotion: and after he was annea-
led, he said oftentymes : *I desire now to go
to enioy my Lord and Sauiour*, and so he
gaue his soule vnto his Creator, about
midnight vpō the first of February 1615.
In all the tyme of his sicknesse although
it were very paynfull, he neuer shewed
the least signe of impatience in the world
nor any feare at all, nor griefe to leaue
his Wife, and Children altogeather vn-
prouided for, and in a strange country,

Y 5   but

but great quietnes of mynd, and conformity with God Almighty his holy will.

5. Exceeding great was the griefe
which generally all did shew when this
newes of his death was published, lamenting on the one side the losse of so
worthy a person whome they entirely
loued, and whose example if God had
giuen him longer life, might haue beene
a potent meanesfor the conuersion of his
Country, whensoeuer he had returned
thereunto againe: and on the other side
comforting themselues, hauing notice
of his holy and happy death, all holding
and esteeming him as a most noble and
worthy Confessour of Christ. He was
buried in the Church of the Society of
Iesus, whose Ghostly child he had alwaies beene. There were present at his
funeralls al the Magistrates of the Citty
both Ecclesiasticall and secular; all the
religious men & the whole Citty, many
kissing his handes in signe of great respect and reuerence. At the taking of his
body out of the house where it lay, there
arose

aroſe a pyous contention who ſhould carry his Coffin, euery one being deſirous to do that office, thereby to honor him. At length it was agreed, that the Lord Gouernour & Iudges ſhould carry it vnto the ſtreet: that then the Citty togeather with the Confraternity of the *Miſericordia* (whereof he was a Brother) ſhould from thence carry it vnto the Church, and that there the Superiors of the religious Orders ſhould take it & conuey it to the place where it was to remaine, during the tyme of the office of the dead.

6. The Cleargy of the Cathedrall Church did celebrate the office both this day, and the day of his ſolemne funerall with great deuotion: the like was done by the religious of the holy orders of *S. Dominicke*, and *S. Francis* in their Monaſteries, and by the Fathers of *S. Auguſtines* Order in the Colledge of the Society; they bringing thither to that end ſuch coſtly ornamentes, and doing all in that fuſhion, as might well haue beſeemed

beseemed the funeralls of a King. Vpon the nynth day after his death all that had beene present at his buriall returned to his funeralls, wherein after the holy sacrifice of the Masse ended, was preached a notable sermon of the heroical vertues of *Don Iusto*, whose Exequies they then solemnized, to the great comfort and edification of all there present, but more in particuler of the *Iapenians*, whereof there were in *Manilla* more then a thousand persons at that tyme, who much reioyced to see those so honoured in a strange country, who for the fayth of Christ were so afflicted and persecuted in their owne.

7 ·   After the death of *Don Iusto*, his wife Daughter, and Grandchildren remayned with a new sorrow and affliction, and *Don Iohn Naytodono* old and sickly with many Children and Grandchildren. *Don Thomas* in like manner, as also the Lady *Iulia* with her Gentlewomen (whereof we spake in the 6. Chapter) all of them in a strange country,

try, not hauing any thing wherewithall
to help themselues . Whereupon the Gouernor *Don Iohn de Silua* with the counsayle and aduise of the Iudges and others
of the Kinges officers, at the petition of
the Citty and religious persons thereof,
did in the name of his Maiesty prouide
them of all thinges necessary for their
sustenance with great liberality , during
the tyme they were to remaine in that
Citty : the which in all those Easterne
partes will be a great praise of the Christian piety , as also of the liberality of his
Catholique Maiesty , who doth so bountifully prouide & carefully defend those
that suffer for the only true and Catholique Religion .

The end of the first Part .

TO THE READER.

I Suppose (good Reader) now that thou hast read the first Part of this Relation, that thou doest desire or expect the second. But indeed as yet I haue not seene it myselfe. I haue written for it into Spayne, vnto my friend which sent me this; and I hope ere longe to'haue it. If I shall vnderstand that by the reading of this thou hast receiued any contentment, it will greatly animate me to take the paynes to translate the other when it commeth. In the meane tyme accept of my good will, and so farewell.

THE

THE TABLE

of the Chapters

THE TABLE.

FINIS.